Self-Management for Actors

Getting Down to (Show) Business

by

Bonnie Gillespie

Cricket Feet Publishing
Los Angeles

Self-Management for Actors: Getting Down to (Show) Business
© 2003 by Bonnie Gillespie
First Edition

Cricket Feet Publishing
P.O. Box 1417
Hollywood, CA 90028
phone/fax: 323.871.1331
http://www.cricketfeet.com
publisher@cricketfeet.com

SCB Distributors
http://www.scbdistributors.com

Unattributed quotations are by Bonnie Gillespie.
Contributed quotations, sections, and photographs are used by permission of the copyright holder, as indicated within.

Cover design by Fabiana Cesa.
Bonnie's headshot by Rod Goodman.
Printed in Canada
LCCN 2003110971
ISBN 0-9723019-7-6

Cricket Feet Publishing titles may be purchased in bulk at special discounts for promotional or educational purposes. Inquiries for sales and distribution, textbook adoption, foreign language translation, editorial, rights and permissions, and future edition inquiries should be addressed as above.

Cricket Feet Publishing is a registered trademark.

What Others Are Saying about Self-Management for Actors

"What a priceless asset for actors to see what really goes on! The chapter on auditioning alone in casting director Bonnie Gillespie's book provides a clear window into some of the good and bad ideas specific actors have brought into the room with them. Invaluable information for the actor!"

—K Callan, actor/author

"At last! Someone who tells it like it *really* is. Bonnie has a handle on this mysterious process of *being* an actor. Note I don't say *acting* as an actor. In addition to being a lucid writer, she is a gifted [former] actor. Bonnie's book is the best demystifying of this wacky industry and a must for every actor, beginning as well as advanced. Brilliant!"

—Joel Colman, director/coach

"What a fantastic resource for actors! Bonnie offers so much valuable information and advice."

—Katy Wallin, CSA casting director/producer

"Bonnie Gillespie's wonderful book should be required reading for all actors! The beginner—needing step-by-step advice for starting the single-proprietor, venture capital business that acting is, and needing How To advice for avoiding missteps—will find that aplenty. The working actor—needing counseling to speed upward career progress—will find page after page of exciting new ideas. It's one of the most clearly detailed, specific example-filled, how-to-do-it-right books available!"

—*Lawrence Parke, Acting World Books*

"For those of you already familiar with Bonnie Gillespie's work, no further comments are even needed. You already know this is a must-have book to understand every aspect of our working industry. For those of you who aren't familiar with her name—congratulations! You're about to receive real insight from one of the most respected members of the business. There's a reason everybody flocks to Bonnie for advice: she knows what she's talking about when it comes to the industry. More importantly—she knows how to articulate and express the thoughts behind the reasons. Through analogies, in-depth interviews, and a fortitude of direct experiences from top experts throughout the industry, every professional element—whether direct or obscure—is exemplified to not only help you survive the industry, but to also increase your successes tenfold. If you seriously want to learn the inside professional workings, you couldn't ask for better guidance. Bonnie will never steer you wrong. *Self-Management for Actors* is an absolute requisite in your arsenal of performer tools."

—*Bill Tarling, actor/author/director of WildOgre.com*

"Preparation and information equal success. This book is the key. Bonnie shares her vast knowledge with you. Her book clarifies and demystifies the casting process. Learn to use your own uniqueness with this helpful guide."

—*Michelle Morris Gertz, CSA*

"Very informative, packed with loads of useful information. Where were you when I started out in the business a hundred years ago?"

—*Baadja-Lyne, actor/writer/poet*

"Bonnie Gillespie's book is insightful, informative, and nurturing. Casting is a difficult process for all involved; ultimately getting the best read or performance from an actor is the goal for everyone. This book should be read by producers as well as actors to make that process as productive and creative as possible."

—*Nancy Meyer, producer/television development executive*

"Bonnie has a great writing style that is fun yet informative while being motivational as well. As a producer of local cable TV spots and industrial videos, I've had many occasions to audition actors who would have benefited greatly from reading this book! *Self-Management for Actors* is a must-read for beginning and intermediate actors. I suspect even very successful actors could learn a thing or two from it while getting a good laugh from some of the horror stories!"

—*Robert Carroll, producer*

"I love the journal entries, the anecdotes, the overall tone of *Self-Management for Actors*. Very welcoming and relaxed while being completely blunt. Awesome! A much-needed book. Most books simply talk about how to pursue an agent or manager—not so much about how to handle and sell yourself."

—*Melanie Mills, actor*

"The business of acting and auditioning can be very intimidating—especially for actors who are just starting out. Bonnie gives the blow-by-blow on what to expect and how to be as prepared as you can. Brilliant advice! Everyone should read this book."

—*Sheila Conlin, casting director/producer*

"What a shame that there are such great actors out there available for film, TV, and theatre who can't be seen by the 'right' people! Well, don't be discouraged. Finally, someone—and it's no secret it's Bonnie Gillespie—has laid out in a clear, concise manner a way for writers, producers, casting directors, and even your own mother to see your work and hire you. Because remember, if we don't see you, you don't get hired. Not even if your mother owns the studio."

—*Mark Troy, playwright/screenwriter*

"What a great resource for actors! The advantages this book gives you are endless. Bonnie's advice and insight will enable you to have the leading edge over many actors. This book is a must-read if you are ready to turn acting into a career, yourself into a professional, and auditions into roles!"

—*Michelle Foumberg, casting director*

"Most actors realize that they must develop their craft. But talent alone is simply not enough to make it in this industry. A skilled actor must also learn how to be an astute marketer and promotional expert. Bonnie offers golden nuggets of valuable and practical advice as to how to go about accomplishing this complicated task. She delightfully illustrates her points with colorful true stories and anecdotes from casting directors and working actors that offer real life insight to this process. If you want to truly succeed in show business, then by all means develop your craft—but also be sure to read Bonnie's book, *Self-Management for Actors*, cover to cover. Believe it or not, the business side of your career can become just as creative and fun as the craft itself, thanks to Bonnie!"

—Glorinda Marie, actor/coach/leader, SF IndieClub

"The author's common sense and good humor make reading this book like having a long chat with an experienced friend in the business. Whether you're just starting out or a seasoned veteran, you will surely find both useful advice and amusingly identifiable anecdotes to keep you motivated and prepared for that next audition. Bonnie Gillespie's smart and savvy expertise smiles through on every page."

—Nelson Aspen, producer/entertainment journalist

"Bonnie Gillespie walks you through the audition process like a dear friend who understands both the craft of acting and the business of casting. She tells you everything you can expect to fully prepare for an audition. Her book is at once instructive, funny, and insightful."

—Kerry Shaw, actor/journalist

"Is acting your passion? Bonnie's comprehensive guide steers you, the actor, in the right direction and helps propel you toward fulfilling your wildest dreams! Bonnie's accurate and high-spirited accounts of the audition process can eliminate much of the mystery while preparing you for an exciting career in the world of entertainment. Reach for the stars!"

—*Pixie Monroe, casting director*

"Just as Bonnie Gillespie's *Casting Qs* has become a must-read by any actor, her new *Self-Management for Actors* should be considered The Actor's Bible. This is a complete eye-opener for both new and established actors. The audition process can be the most nerve-racking experience, but Bonnie reminds us that by following a few simple steps and being prepared, actors can walk away as winners—even if we don't get the part. Los Angeles can be a tough town, but this book can help all actors survive it."

—*TL Kolman, managing director of the Attic Theatre, SAG/AEA*

"*Self-Management for Actors* should be required reading for all beginning actors. It takes all the guesswork out of the business and replaces it with solid, honest, valuable information. A blueprint masterpiece on the total process!"

—*Donnice Wilson, manager/producer*

"Bonnie has done her homework. Her interest in demystifying the process for actors is to the advantage of every casting director from Hollywood to Dublin. We can only hope that actors read this book. Thanks, Bonnie!"

—*Mark Paladini, CSA, UCLA Extension film and TV casting instructor*

"One is truly hard-pressed these days to find a writer who is as actor-friendly and as knowledgeable as Bonnie Gillespie. Having worked on both sides of the industry (as actor and casting director), she makes it her business to empower the working actor to be professional. This book is for those special actors who simply refuse to see themselves as underdogs in the casting hierarchy, and who want to build respected professional reputations while remaining true to their art."

—*Frances Uku, actor*

"This book is amazing! Successful actors at all levels truly understand that this is a business and that—in order to get to where you want to go—you have to be able to do some of the work yourself. What Bonnie has put together with *Self-Management for Actors* is a blueprint from which to build your business plan and grow toward reaching your career goals as an actor."

—*Mitchell Fink, actor*

"Bonnie infuses her book with detailed, straightforward, and accurate information in a lighthearted, easy-to-take-to-heart way. Most of this business is common sense, peppered with the occasional there-are-no-rules, there-are-the-exceptions. If you want to act, please be in it for the long haul. Just know—if you hang in there long enough—you will eventually get work."

—*Elisa Goodman, CSA, Goodman/Edelman Casting*

"A delightfully earnest roadmap of common sense, helpful tips, and insightful casting director advice for new actors seeking a guide for the everyday acting process!"

—*Angela Bertolino & Carla Lewis, Hollywood OS*

"Why aren't you working as an actor? Because you haven't finished reading this book! Voila! The ultimate step-by-step guide to success in the industry! I've witnessed many superior actors fall by the wayside simply because they lacked the self-management skills described in Bonnie's book. There is no reason to find yourself adrift in the industry when you have expert guidance at your fingertips. *Self-Management for Actors: Getting Down to (Show) Business* is that guide. All the actor has to do is follow the directions. Simple! Bonnie is well researched, intuitive, and wise beyond her years. Believe her, prepare, and follow your dreams."

—Lynn Stallings, director/producer/coach

"I swear Bonnie Gillespie is Emerson reincarnate. If you've never read Emerson's essays 'Self-Reliance' and 'The Over-Soul,' you should. Then add to that this book of Bonnie's and you should soon find yourself a formidable competitor in one of the most competitive businesses out there: professional acting. The clarity with which Bonnie takes you through the process of auditioning is alone worth the price of admission. You can't miss with Self-Management for Actors. It is page after page of good solid common sense insight with tons of quotes from casting directors, actors, and industry professionals. It answers many 'I always wondered about that' questions."

—Robert Brody, Showfax/Screenplay Online/Sides Express

"Bonnie Gillespie has the best hair in Hollywood!"

—José Eber, celebrity stylist

For all the actors,
no matter who manages them.

Table of Contents

Foreword

Shortly after receiving my MFA in acting I came to the realization I was not particularly interested in the gypsy life of a regional theatre actor—I needed roots. The four people in the world that have ever heard me sing will tell you that Broadway wasn't the answer. I had been told, however, that my "unique look" (a nice euphemism for being called weird-looking) might be well-suited for film and television. Everything was settled. I moved to Los Angeles in 1992 with the intention of pursuing a career in film and television and perhaps doing some supplemental theatre to prevent any "artistic stagnation."

I had received excellent training at a well-regarded institution. I had played clowns and villains, lunatics and straight men. I also vaguely remember wearing rope sandals and some kind of tunic but that memory is foggy. I was a good actor with a professional attitude and an interesting character face. How could Hollywood resist? Well, they were about to show me.

I'm embarrassed to admit it now, but I thought it would be relatively easy. I was sure that reputable talent agents all over town would be clamoring for a well-trained theatre actor, particularly one with no film credits and some tunic/sandal thingy on his resumé. I was convinced that the doors to casting offices would swing open and scripts would be handed to me from all angles. What I recognize now as absurd cockiness (or at least naïveté) is in some ways attributable to the Ivory Tower mentality of so many BFA and MFA programs. We are taught there that it is all about *craft.* If you have the talent and work on your voice and movement and rehearse your monologue enough times, then you will win the role. There are 28-year-olds all over the country playing King Lear. And some are doing it very well. What we don't realize at the time is that we are competing in a talent pool of 15 to 50 people. Most of them within a 10-year age range. Audition slots are guaranteed; all you need to do is pick a time and sign up. What I discovered after moving to Los Angeles is that I was competing with 10,000 people just to *meet* the person who *might* sign me and subsequently *try* to get me an audition. It was a whole new ball game.

I don't mean to disparage these programs at all. They are invaluable and I applaud every actor that devotes his time and energy to the honing of his craft. I do believe, however, that many programs are remiss in teaching the realities of the business, particularly with regard to the world of film and television. When an actor leaves school he is a *manufacturer* of a product (good acting). When he arrives in Los Angeles, he needs to learn to *sell* the product. As with any industry, manufacturing and sales require very different skill sets. I know many actors here who have a marvelous product but little ability to sell it. Conversely, I know lots and lots (and lots) of actors who are terrific salesmen but their product sorta stinks.

When an actor arrives in Los Angeles, he is hopefully the manufacturer of a good product, but many actors soon discover that there is a steep learning curve on the sales end. It can be extremely frustrating to know that you have a good product and find that nobody will even consider "buying" it. This frustration can lead to great bitterness and many good actors will "jump ship" before their time. I personally spent four years in a muffin factory. Although I look superb in a hairnet, I would have been quite content to cut those four years to one or two!

This is where Bonnie's book comes in. I believe it is geared towards actors that have some real training and a strong sense of craft but need to know how to transition into the "sales" arena. This book will teach every actor how to efficiently and effectively market himself as an actor which can mean shaving years off the learning curve and saying good-bye to that crummy temp job just a little bit sooner.

—Bob Clendenin
SAG/AFTRA/AEA
ex-muffin employee

Introduction

A manager is a great asset to your career—at the right time. Too soon or too late and you could make a few mistakes in either direction from which recovery could be difficult, in terms of the long-haul of your career. There is plenty of work to do *before* signing with a manager or agent. That's where *Self-Management for Actors* comes in.

Casting directors generally do not care *at all* where headshots and resumés come from if you are the right actor for the role at the exact moment they need you. Commercial casting directors in particular are keen on finding new talent or looks that aren't currently represented on TV.

Where it becomes more difficult to get seen without representation is for big films and regular-season TV shows. Casting directors on these assignments rely heavily on their relationships with agents and managers. These folks don't simply seek submissions of actors' headshots and resumés from agents and managers; they seek well-thought-out recommendations based on relationships cultivated over years of experience. Therefore, I *do* recommend that actors find representation as soon as it's practical.

Meanwhile, marketing is a toughie for many actors. One of my biggest pet peeves with formal acting training is that it concentrates too much on the craft and not much *at all* on the business. Since actors must navigate the waters of both craft and marketing, I think a major disservice has been done when someone completes a degree in *acting*, but has not had one class in the *business* of acting.

For an overview of the business side of this industry, spend some time doing research. You can even stand right in the aisles of Samuel French, Larry Edmunds, or Take One bookstores and skim a few books. Attend every free panel discussion, seminar, or class audit that you can find. Information shared at these events—while more limited than what may exist in ongoing classes—is often both valuable and motivational.

Take classes wherever you feel the most comfortable or the most challenged. Work out parts of your craft you haven't explored yet and make sure that you always audit classes before signing up for the long haul. Auditing ensures that you connect with the instructor and allows you to talk over the classes with current and former students to make sure the classes are a good fit to your needs. Don't get in a rut with any one instructor or technique. Explore your options and have fun!

Be excited that you are living your life as a working actor. The work is more than what you do on a set. Stay motivated every day! As you learn to market yourself, if you're not excited about that process, how can anyone else be? It *is* overwhelming. I know! I've seen many really talented actors burn out from trying to keep up with the business end of things. It's not an easily-developed skill, but handling the business of acting is something I was always very good at, back when I was acting. So, even though I've retired from performing, I want to share some marketing tips and self-management plans with you. In the pages that follow, I will help break it all down into a process that is easier to follow and less intimidating than it appears when you're on your own, looking at the many business-related tasks all at once.

That's my goal: to present information in such a way that people think, "Man! Why didn't I think of that?" Then I want to see you move forward with the advice in little steps and, hopefully, remember to shout out a thank you to me when you accept your Oscar. Not too much to ask, is it?

Another request I have is that you keep me posted on how things go for you (contact info is inside the front cover). I love to keep up with the progress of actors. It helps me give better advice when I know what is working for you and what snags may have come up along the way.

Just remember that there is nothing magic or even a little mystical about the business side of the business (or even about the craft, if you look at the academic science of it). There is, however, a cloak of protection around some industry information. As one casting director once told me, "This is *not* classified information! Most of it is common sense and the rest of it is all available through research." Sure. But as an artist, you are trying very hard to balance the muse that helps you create, the inspiration that keeps you going, and the organizational skills that allow you to navigate it all. Oh yes, and you're trying not to take it personally, when you don't get cast! Forget about keeping all those proverbial balls in the air at once. Reward yourself for each success you have in the complex life that is the actor's.

Please note, throughout this book, that any specific mention of a company is simply that: a mention. I have not been paid to represent any company or service in good favor and you should make no assumption as to the reputation of such companies and services. Additionally, the information provided herein does not represent, on the part of myself nor the publishing company, a recipe for success, a guarantee of a job, or even a promise of increased confidence in audition situations. Application is up to you!

Finally, you'll notice that I have chosen to refer to casting directors using the female pronoun. This is not due to some feminist agenda, but due to the fact that casting is one of the only female-dominated segments of the entertainment industry. In an attempt to balance the scales a bit, I have chosen to refer to actors, agents, and managers using the male pronoun.

Please enjoy *Self-Management for Actors*. If you have borrowed this book from a friend and would like one of your own, please flip to the back of the book for an order form or visit CricketFeet.com.

Acknowledgments

Almost every piece of advice in this book started out as an answer to a question posed by an actor (aspiring or working). Without actors who felt comfortable enough to ask important questions about the process of self-management, this book would not exist. Thank you to all of the actors who have led the way for the development of this concept and this book.

The tireless good will and inspirational words of Lawrence Parke and Robert Brody have kept me focused and excited about this process all along. And the unconditional acceptance into their ranks I have received from casting directors has been truly amazing to behold. To find family in your work is always unexpected. What a delightful year this has turned out to be!

Although I no longer write for *Back Stage West*, I would be remiss were I not to acknowledge the support and encouragement I continue to receive from Lori Talley, Dany Margolies, Rob Kendt, Thomas Mills, and Rosa Fernandez. You truly are the heart and soul of what *Back Stage West* aspires to be.

Thank you to the actors, casting directors, agents, managers, writers, and photographers who contributed to this book. Most of all, I am grateful to Bob Clendenin for his spirited and delightful foreword. I am proud to know you and to call you my friend.

I must express my gratitude to authors Deborah Jacobson and Dan Poynter, whose advice shone the light upon my path. And a tremendous debt of gratitude exists to all the actors who pre-ordered this book—before I had even finished writing it—based on their assessment of my work in *Casting Qs: A Collection of Casting Director Interviews.* To all of the professors whose recommendations caused my books to now exist on your college and university bookshelves, I truly appreciate you for expanding the world of an actor's academic training.

Thank you to my family and friends, specifically, Faith Salie (my precious cousin), Art Weaver, Dawn VanDercreek, Judy Kerr, Paul Molinaro, and my many online friends at Wolfesden.net, WildOgre.com, and Yahoo! group Somesuch-Whatnot. I sincerely appreciate the research and feedback provided by Ali Sowels, Rose Auerbach, Joni Harbin, Kenny French, and Brandt Stevens. And a *very* special thank you goes out to Jamie Caples, Mary Torio, Elizabeth Johnson-Stevens, Aaron Silverman, and Kerry Shaw, without whom this book would've never left my house.

Finally, I humbly admit that I owe so much to my partner Keith Johnson. Your faith in me has resulted in far more than this book and the one before it. For all of the bounty, the lessons, and the trust, I am forever grateful. For having followed my instincts when Mom sent you to me, I am proud.

Part One: Mindset

What's Important?

A healthy mindset is perhaps the most important element to a working actor's ability to self-manage. There will be times you will have to work "outside yourself" in order to be your own best advisor. A manager or an agent will have a vision of how to market you that you may not see for yourself. And if you're on your own, you'll definitely need to check in with others at times. While self-management is a term that implies you do it all for yourself, there certainly will be ample opportunity for you to consult with experts and peers. So, make sure you have a mindset that allows for constructive criticism without interpreting such feedback as an ego-shattering blow.

How best to do that? Remember that your acting career is, in fact, a business. Some people will recommend that actors see themselves as products, with the casting director as the shopper, the producer as the buyer, the agent or manager as the marketing director for the product, and the audience as the product's consumer. If that analogy works for you, by all means, go with it. I will simply state that you are operating a business every day and that that requires not only the lovely creative mind that allows you to embody other characters, but also the organizational skills of a successful business owner. If the idea of becoming organized or developing managerial skills repulses you, then self-management is not for you. You will simply need to rely on luck, talent, and timing to have your creative dreams realized. Those who self-manage, though, will have the added benefit of a certain level of control over their own career paths (and that's more than just controlling whether you used staples or glue to attach your headshot to your resumé).

I think marketing is a major part of an actor's success. Yes, of course, there's craft, there's raw talent, there's a look, there's luck... but there is so much more staying power among those with business sense and marketing savvy. It really can give you an edge over someone else who may be on par with you in every other element.

Breaking It Down

Many actors have asked me to assess—based on my many interviews with casting directors—what factor has the most impact on whether an actor is called in for an audition over another actor. Is it training? Look? Special skills? Union status? Credits? Agency representation? I like to answer that question with a quip shared by CSA soap opera casting director Mark Teschner during a panel discussion I moderated. When asked what the *one* most important factor for getting called in was, Teschner responded, "Shirt color!" And what is that shirt color? "Blue." Of course, that's a joke, but it really does summarize the way casting directors feel about the minutiae actors tend to place emphasis on, when dissecting the "call-in" elements.

There is no *one* thing. There are so many things—and there are no things—that make the difference in whether a certain actor is called in for an audition. So, rather than focusing on breaking down those elements, which differ based on who you ask, I'd like to focus on breaking down things actors control... shirt color being one of them, of course!

I am a recovering academic and would *love* to apply science (or at least empirical statistical analysis) to the casting process. Sadly, it is *so* much more of a "gut instinct" than anything else. Casting directors take a look at your headshot and say, "Yep. That's the *type* we need. Ooh, there's something going on in the eyes. There's a life there." Then they flip the headshot over and start skimming the credits. "Hmm. He's worked with so-and-so. She's a great director! Oh, trained with what's-his-name. Ooh! Improv! That's great. He's repped by this-and-that-agency. Super! We have a relationship with them. Call him in!"

Getting called in is much less about any one thing and much more about an overall *feeling* the casting director gets when she first sees your headshot. That's why everything should come across extremely sharp, really clean, and clearly representative of your type.

As for what means the *most*, it's got to be a common experience. Relationships are everything, and if you've studied with, worked with, or are repped by someone with whom the casting director has a connection, you're a lot closer to "in" than you might imagine.

So, don't focus on what might be the most "weighted" item in your resumé. Focus instead on putting together an overall package that you can be proud of and that you feel *really* represents you accurately. Your "vibe" should come through all of it. After that, it's just a matter of that vibe connecting to something in the casting director.

In presenting that vibe, how important is the headshot itself? Remember, you are trying to gain entry into a world with that headshot. Make it great. More importantly, make it *real*. *Every* casting director says how important it is that you look like your headshot.

So, is a good headshot important? Yes. Is it even more important that the headshot looks like you? Yes. Can a headshot get you in the door? *Yes*. Do credits matter? Yes... but remember, your headshot will be looked at first. I don't know a single casting director who *first* looks at a resumé and *then* flips it over to see if the headshot is of any interest to her.

Does representation matter? Sure. If you are signed with a great agent who has a fantastic relationship with a casting director who just *happens* to be looking for your type *right now* and who happens to call your agent, asking for a list of the talent of your type she represents, then yes: your representation just got you in the door. But, since I'm assuming you're working on the whole self-management concept *because* you don't have that perfect agent with that perfect relationship at that perfect moment (not yet anyway), I'll continue with the rest of what matters.

You want to be sure your envelope is opened when it arrives in a casting director's office. The *best* way to be sure that happens? Make connections in the industry. Network. Meet people who know people who know people and invest in those relationships. Truly, the best way to send an envelope that gets opened is to respond to a request by someone in the know.

So, you're now connecting with people who work in casting and you learn that a fellow casting colleague has mentioned a new project for which you'd be perfect. Your contact calls you and says, "Get your headshot over to so-and-so's office and tell her I sent you." Need an agent to make that happen? No way.

Back to what's most important, one of my favorite analogies on the weight various elements have in getting an actor called in comes from a wonderfully talented Los Angeles actor named Robin Gwynne.

Your submission envelope nominates you (agency submissions are like belonging to the right political party, a much stronger nomination). Your headshot seconds the nomination. Your cover letter is your campaign speech. Your resumé votes you into office. Your audition is your term. Callbacks are how you're doing in the polls. Booking the job is your re-election. Once you're an incumbent, it's easier to stay in office. A string of jobs is your career.

Remember, there will always be the next job and the next job and the next job. Don't ever focus on how much you could be doing "if only" you had an agent, "if only" you had league school training, "if only" you were taller. You should always be moving forward to the next opportunity, staying on schedule to achieve certain benchmark goals. Then suddenly you'll notice that you aren't missing any opportunities because you have everything you need ready to pounce on every opportunity you hear about. You're involved in a process.

What's My Type?

Casting directors put out character breakdowns to agents and managers asking for specific *types* of actors to fill roles from the script. It's always good business sense to know, as an actor, what your type is. That way, when you see a casting notice or hear about a role, you'll know whether your type has a chance of meshing with the type called for.

What are some of the more commonly called-for types in Hollywood? Read on. Keep in mind that these lists are by no means exhaustive, as someone can always come up with a new type in describing a character.

Typical Types

Young Males
bad boy
boy-next-door
nerdy kid
bully
quirky/trendy
smart-ass
jock
brain

paste-eater (less cool than the nerdy kid, who has the potential to develop a new piece of software before starting college. The paste-eater will only develop a coated tongue.)

<u>Young Females</u>
princess
girl-next-door
trendsetter
bully
jock
brain
awkward/gawky
ingénue (the young, fresh-faced innocent that the boys want to win over and the audience is rooting for in most classic tales)

<u>Adult Males</u>
leading man
the nice guy
that creepy weird guy
jock
blue-collar worker
cop/career military
executive
lawyer/politician
teacher/professor
dad
computer genius
salesman
slacker
doctor/nurse
jokester
player
slimy con man

criminal/thug/heavy
artist/poet/musician

<u>Adult Females</u>
leading lady
her best friend
bimbo/airhead
jock
sex goddess
cop
executive/lawyer/politician
social climber/bitch
teacher/professor
mom
frustrated housewife
saleswoman
doctor/nurse
wacky neighbor
criminal
artist/poet/musician
late-start careerist

<u>Older Actors</u>
empty-nester
grandparent
judge
religious leader
codger/senile

Keep in mind that people love to classify types by creating hybrids. Example: "I need a young, hip, dancing Helen Hunt type," yields, say, Julia Stiles. It's just easier for people to take a known commodity and tweak it to their current needs. What would your hybrid type be?

I recommend that you watch TV, watch commercials,

and see plays and films with a little notepad (in mind, if not in hand). You'll see what the types are and be able to determine what type you are. Always note which roles are the ones *you* would've auditioned for, if not the roles in which you'd be cast. Obviously, if any of the roles are ones for which you *have* auditioned and some other type got cast, you were called in against the type they were going to end up casting.

Pay attention to the roles you're given in acting class. Don't be too weirded out by reading parts in class that are "against type." One of the goals in class is to push your boundaries in an attempt to stretch your range. So, even if something is very much *not* your type, go ahead and give it your all. You may surprise yourself. Of course, that's an in-class thing. When it comes to an audition, you first must be the "right" type to get called in, and then you must deliver the goods. Confidence will help with that (even if your type is "under-confident nerd" or something like that). Knowing who you are and where your strengths are will make your performance that much stronger.

Play your look and be yourself.

Type Me Please

One of my favorite activities is helping actors discover their types. It is so important for an actor to know his type, in order to do proper marketing, yet it's nearly impossible for an actor to determine his own type without some sort of outside assistance. In fact, if you're currently represented, your agent or manager should help determine your marketing goals, and that includes type. What follows are a few examples of "typing" that I've done for various actors, along with their headshots and some feedback from the actors on whether the typing exercises are accurate.

photo by Rob Martin

Canadian actor Jessica Van Dusen heard everything from "high school senior" to "young mom" and from "psycho ex-girlfriend" to "girl-next-door" using her current headshots. "I don't want to be auditioning for mom roles if I look like I'm in high school," she told me. "It'd be so nice to have an agent determine what I'd be best submitted for."

When I typed Jessica, I realized, if she's *consistently* hearing that she's "high school" when she shows up for "young mom" roles, then that's a good clue as to what she should try and market. Plenty of adult actors play high school roles.

Here's what I get from her headshot: sassy, sarcastic, smart-ass, vixen type. This would be the girl that steals the lead's boyfriend or the one who is scheming to take over the sorority. I don't see her "reading" young enough to play high school, from this headshot. She looks more college-aged to me. Also, she doesn't look old enough (or wholesome enough, frankly) to do "young mom." This headshot really is putting out a vibe closer to "psycho ex-girlfriend" (as she put it) than to "girl-next-door." Of course, that's all from that one photo, and a lot depends on how she "reads" when she goes into the room.

Now, before I get too deep into the typing exercises, I'll share a warning I received from a casting director friend of mine, who saw me offering this "service" to actors, based on their headshots alone.

Establishing type from a headshot is of questionable value, at best, since one doesn't know if the headshot is accurately conveying your persona. In some cases, what the person actually needs is new headshots since the ones they have misrepresent or underplay their true character strengths.

With that warning in mind, I'll now share a story about how I discovered my type, back when I was still pursuing acting. My first on-camera class as an adult was a very telling experience. I'd been marketing myself as the kid I'd been rather than the adult actor I'd grown into. It's hard to know something like that, but it's *so* much better when you do know it—even if you have to hear it from someone else. Rather than focusing on the type you know—in your heart—that you *are*, focus on the type you *seem* to others. I know it's not fair, but being in sync with your presented image will make marketing yourself much easier.

I was in a four-week class with a casting director at one of those workshop places a few years back. I was, prior to that class, pretty sure of how I came across on camera and in my work, and my marketing plan reflected that. I was working plenty as a college kid type, but not as much as I did after "the incident."

During one class session, the casting director left our headshots on a chair in the room before the break. She'd been sitting near me while we were watching each actor read audition sides. At the break, I looked over to my headshot, which was resumé-side-up. There was a notation on the resumé (as is common practice. Casting directors will make notes to themselves of their first impression of actors, so their memories will be "jogged" after it's been a while since meeting the actors). It read, "Good ol' gal."

I was devastated!

"Good ol' gal?" Hell no! Not me! I am elegant and statuesque and voluptuous and funny and brilliant! I am *not* some "good ol' gal!"

Then I took a good hard look at myself (this is where it gets important to distinguish *the type you are* from *the type you seem* when someone *first* meets you) and realized, "My goodness! I am an Atlantan, through and through. I am not a *Cosmo* Girl. I am not a Valley Girl. I am a Southern Belle but I am also one of the guys. I shoot pool, I throw darts, I bowl, I drink, and I am cynical and sarcastic. The most formal thing I own is the pair of jeans *without* a hole in the knee. Y'know what? Maybe I *am* a good ol' gal!"

Holy cow! That changed everything. Suddenly, by not fighting what everyone was already seeing in me, I started booking like mad! Once I stopped resisting what was *most* marketable about my look, I was able to go out for the roles I was more likely to book.

So, brace yourself and really listen to what others are telling you. Look at your resumé and see what sort of roles you keep booking. Then run like the wind with that piece of information tucked in soundly. It's going to really help, in the long run.

Yes, it *is* possible to market yourself in as many ways as you feel "castable," but know that you will need headshots that support each of these *types* and you'll *have* to know for which type you've been called in before you audition, so you'll make sure you're in the right frame of mind, style of dress, and so on.

I'd say it's far easier to pick your big strength and embrace it. If you find it's not working after a year of solid marketing attempts to that end, then it's time for a re-evaluation of type or even a type makeover (see *Reinvention*, next chapter).

I know it is *far* more valuable for an actor to know the type he is when he enters the room—the type he *plays*—than the type his headshot says he is, but casting directors look at headshots every day without knowing the actor pictured. There is quite a bit of decision-making going on before the actor ever even has the chance of getting into the room to audition.

So, no, I can't tell an actor I've never met what type he *is*, but I sure can tell him what type his *headshot* is saying he is. If it's off the mark from the type he *is*, it's time for a new headshot. I'd call that kind of information helpful. It is a gift to know who you are, truly. Your self-awareness will permeate everything you do, and that's a big plus for your acting—no matter what your type may be.

Nancy Onorato, a New Jersey actor, is so vibrant. She has a wonderful look that should get her called in for 18 to 24 roles, probably leading lady, really sincere and direct without much of an edge to the character or agenda to the delivery.

There is definitely some "sexy" in there, but it's not the primary element. Nancy's headshot sells sort of a young Laura San Giacomo (*Just Shoot Me*) or even Lindsay Korman

(*Passions*) vibe—much more direct than smoldering, in terms of appeal. Nancy can tap into leading lady roles more than the "wacky neighbor" or "smart-ass" little sister. I wouldn't have Nancy push toward "bitchy executive" with this headshot.

photo by Jeffrey Hornstein

Nancy let me know that both her acting coach and photographer agree that this is her best shot; fresh, good for facial cleanser commercials or even blue jeans. Turns out that Nancy is older than her age range would indicate, and worries that she won't be taken seriously because she looks so young. My take on that topic is that being a good actor is what gets you taken seriously. The rest of it is just the role the casting directors want you to play. They may see a high school student, but if you can pull it off, so be it!

When I mentioned Lindsay Korman to Nancy, she let me know that she couldn't see herself being "mean enough" to work on soaps. Of course, there are good girls on soaps too. They have to cry pretty (not like me with the big red nose) and are often in damsel-in-distress storylines, but they're there.

photo by Eric Jacobs

Kathryn Johnston, a New York actor who has recently moved to the ever-expanding market of the southeast, is a member of SAG and AEA. Her commercial headshot is really great. It gives off the vibe of a teenager's mom (ala *Gilmore Girls*). Commercially, she could do ads for dish soap, satellite dish installation, and high-end luxury cars. In fact, her look is very marketable right now.

Her angular theatrical shot is really sexy. She has a scandalous look to her, similar to Jacqueline Bisset's character in the 1982 feature film *Class*. Sexy, but troubled;

classy, yet dangerous. Kathryn has a lot of theatre (legit stage) experience and this headshot is versatile enough to use for stage *or* theatrical (film and episodic television) submissions. Kathryn could expect a favorable response to this headshot for MOWs or series for Lifetime or the Oxygen network. It's the Valerie Bertinelli stage of life, for Kathryn, and there is certainly no shortage of work there!

photo by Eric Jacobs

Christopher Behrens, an actor and writer who has recently relocated to Los Angeles from Northern California, has a great character look, especially in his serious headshot. A smiling shot, while nice commercially, isn't really going to get Christopher into many casting offices. It's not the image he'll sell, once he arrives in person, so the conflicting messages won't serve him well. This is where a "mini" headshot on the resumé side of the headshot is a good call. It would show that Christopher does have nice teeth and a great smile, without distracting anyone from the "heavy" he will likely read for.

photo by Matthew Cowell

Christopher confirmed that he usually reads for the role of the villain, the cop, or the detective. He knows he's not selling "boy-next-door" in any headshot, no matter how hard he tries. While trying to get noticed for leading man roles, Christopher should go with his strengths: get called in for the role of the "heavy," then impress the casting directors with his "breakout potential." It certainly is possible to be the bad guy *and* the leading man—especially over the age of 30—but the best way to prove he is capable of such roles is for Christopher to get some leading theatre roles under his belt. Good reviews in leading man roles on stage will get him called in for film and TV roles for which he normally wouldn't be considered.

photo by Rod Goodman

Los Angeles actor and SAG and AFTRA member Richard Eck, on the other hand, is the classic everyman. He has a versatile look, tends to play heroic cop roles. He doesn't get called in for edgy cops, such as those on *NYPD Blue* or

The Shield, but rather for the guest-star cop roles on series ranging from *Malcolm in the Middle* to *Passions* and from *Roswell* to *The Division*. While Richard has chiseled good looks and broad shoulders, he has found more success in supporting roles than lead characters—so far.

Richard has begun selling his "cop type" with this casual, yet detective-style 3/4 headshot by Rod Goodman. This headshot tends to result in very specific calls and bookings for Richard, whereas his less-specific non-cop headshot sometimes missed the mark on submissions for cop roles. The dark clothing, conservative stance, and serious facial expression in this headshot tell casting directors exactly what they need to know about Richard: "I have a 'cop' look." Then, upon looking at Richard's resumé, casting directors are assured that he has consistently performed in cop roles and they bring Richard in. Once his relationship with these casting directors builds, he will be brought in for larger roles—or perhaps the lead role in some new cop series down the line. Meanwhile, Richard is taking advantage of marketing his type as it seems to sell best, knowing it is all part of building his career.

How Important Is Knowing Your Type?

Those of you who doubt how big a deal knowing how to market yourself is to casting directors, take heed: it's serious. Knowing your type, marketing yourself correctly, and looking like your headshot make all the difference. Look at it this way: you are in *any* other business. You get business cards printed up. There is a misprint and your name is misspelled and your job title is incorrect. Are you going to hand out these business cards as if they represent you correctly? Of course not! Yet actors do that *every* day by using headshots that do not look like them or that do not properly represent their dominant type. This misrepresentation pretty much means the headshot is selling a person the actor cannot deliver when he shows up in the flesh. And while actors are busy trying to get jobs the "wrong" headshots would lead to, the actors could be losing jobs the headshots that *look* like them—in their dominant type— would help them get.

If you're not seeing patterns from your own history of work, the best way to ascertain your type is to request that people in the know (agents, managers, casting directors, photographers, publicists, coaches, even fellow actors) take a look at your headshot, take a look at you, and give you a list of the first five adjectives that come to mind. You can also ask these folks whether your headshot is off the mark in portraying you the way you really come off in person.

Take all of those opinions and look at the words that top the lists the most often. If that's who you are, when you show up for an audition, then that's how to market yourself. If the type you appear to be, upon this survey process, is really far from the roles you tend to book, then you'd better get some more representative headshots, to increase the likelihood that you get called in for the roles of your type.

Once you know your type, you'll be much better at submitting yourself for roles. Remember: watch all TV shows, commercials, films, and plays with a critical eye toward, "Which role is mine?" Not which one you could play if they had "gone another way," but which role is the one being played by an actor in your category and age range. What role would *you* have been up for? Market to that type and *then* convince people to take risks on you—as you branch out to other roles and other types.

Playing Your Look

I surveyed casting directors from Los Angeles to New York, and from Canada to Chicago. Although a few casting directors asked to speak "off the record" about their opinions of an actor's *look*, quite a few were eager to share perspective on what—about a look—is important to the casting process.

How Actors Should Show up for Auditions

"For theatrical auditions, you should dress for the role or the suggestion of the character, but you don't need to be in costume. For commercials on the other hand, [casting directors] love you to come in costume," explained Gennette Tondino, who casts feature films.

"Actors should show up as close to character as possible," suggests New York film casting director and former actor Maria Greco. And if there is no specific instruction? "Upscale casual is always safe. That means clean, neat, nice clothes. Not ripped jeans and clothes that look as though they have been slept in." Greco continued, "It amazes me that actors come to an audition with so little respect for themselves as well as [us]."

"I don't recommend wearing a costume, because it sends a message that the actor doesn't fully trust that we'll recognize their talent unless they have a nurse's outfit on," opined CSA casting director Mark Paladini, who casts films and episodic television. "It's even worse when it's worn for the director and producer who have already hired a professional costume designer. A director once told me, 'I always know the actor dressed like a cop won't get the job. The costume is in place of something that is missing in the talent department,'" Paladini shared.

Ponderosa casting director Richard De Lancy conveyed the most common response among casting directors, by saying actors should show up dressed, "Nice casual. If you're coming in for an attorney, dress more like an attorney than showing up in beachwear."

"Dress your best," requested New York film and video

casting director Jeffrey Arsenault. "That is not the same to an actor as it is to someone in the corporate world. Dress in clean, comfortable clothing—and it should look like it was put on clean that morning, not last Saturday night. When in doubt, think *soap opera.* I frown upon actors dressing in character unless they are specifically told to do so."

"Don't dress in character. If you are auditioning for a doctor, don't wear a white coat with a stethoscope around your neck," Lori Cobe-Ross—who casts the PBS series *On Common Ground* as well as independent films—advised. "We want to see your acting ability and not your wardrobe. Sometimes my reception area looks like an audition for the Village People! I hate that because acting—not wardrobe— is your job."

A *don't* from Los Angeles features casting director Matthew Barry, CSA, is about respect. "Don't be late, don't stink up our office with your overabundance of cologne, and don't have your cell phone ringing." Otherwise, he suggested, "If you're playing a cop, don't show up in a T-shirt. If you're playing a toughie, don't show up in a button-down. A doctor's smock does not convince us, 'Hey, he looks just like a doctor in that smock.'"

While most casting directors believe it is more important to *suggest* the character than to show up *in character* for an audition, there are those who want to see you in costume. However, it is more important to most casting directors that actors *feel* that they are the character, and for some actors, clothing helps make that happen.

Chicago CSA casting director Jane Alderman (*The Straight Story, Love Jones, Early Edition*) advised, "I feel actors should come in clothing and shoes that help them feel appropriate for the part and that gives everyone the allusion of this character." An anonymously-participating Los Angeles casting director echoed the importance of being appropriate. "If the part is a doctor, trousers and a shirt are a better choice than flip-flops and cutoffs."

Jackie Lind, who recently completed location casting in Canada for the feature *Open Range*, indicated that an actor should "suggest the role. You don't need to bang us over the head with it." She also noted an important element of on-camera auditions: "Stay away from visually distracting clothing like black, white, stripes, and logos."

Beyond showing up in costume is the element of showing up in character. "I am always impressed when an actor shows up to an audition in character. Nothing more says, 'This part is *mine.*' to me," explained Los Angeles indie feature casting director Caprisha Smyles.

Dino Ladki, who has cast several episodics for MTV and runs TheCastList.com, coined a term that nailed down the feeling of most casting directors on the subject. "Show up *in-character-esque.* Don't show up dressed like a drug addict to audition for the prom queen. I think a good rule of thumb is *actor casual.* Don't make a big deal one way or the other because you're likely to get pegged," he said.

"I would like to hire an actor who can portray the character and who can step outside of the character's needs to converse as a professional actor," Stephen Snyder—who casts commercials, indies, and music videos—revealed. "That way, we can talk intelligently about the adjustments and character information. As far as clothing, anything that is over-the-top is not needed. We do have some imagination and we know how to use it."

Conveying Your Primary Look

"Know that you can't have just one look in person. Actors have a thousand souls inside them," mused Alderman. She suggested a maximum of two different headshot looks, as there is no way to capture an actor's every look. Other casting directors agree that "it's helpful to have a few different headshots to convey different character types," but that there is no need to go overboard.

The primary comment from casting directors was the importance of actors looking like their headshots. "If I've not met the actor," explained De Lancy, "then the photograph is what they're selling. That is exactly what I am expecting in the room. That's what I called in."

"If you look like your pictures, you should be fine," speculated Cobe-Ross. "I had an actress come in for a lead in a movie. She had a terrific headshot and really looked the part. When she came in, I was in shock. She weighed at least 150 pounds more in person. I told her she needed new pictures and she told me that they *were* new pictures. What a great photo-retoucher she used!"

Paladini suggested that an accurate headshot is essential, but that casting directors do understand subtle changes. "Stubble comes and goes based on current bookings, but the picture should not be drastically different from what the actor looks like. Agents should let us know when the appointment is made if the actor's hair is a totally different color or length—or missing completely!"

"Any photo more than two years old is out—no matter how much work you are getting from it," Arsenault insisted. "Using the same photo for too long can send the message that you've been in the same place too long. You want casting directors to think you are always growing. Please don't send me a photo with a note saying, 'By the way, now my hair is blond, I have a full beard, and I lost 30 pounds.'"

Mistakes Actors Make

"The only mistake I ever find with actors is that they just show up, without paying attention whatsoever to their looks," noted Alderman. On the flip-side, De Lancy believes actors try too hard. "Come in with your day-to-day look unless you are told to show up in something specific. The more natural you look, the better," De Lancy said. Ladki agreed, noting that "severity—one way or the other" is the biggest mistake regarding an actor's look.

"I find that a lot of women come in without makeup, especially when the role calls for something more glamorous. I don't understand why they want to do that," Tondino lamented. "Most of the time the director or producer looks at the photo and looks at the actor and can't believe it's the same person. If the role says 'attractive,' let us see that. If the role says, 'great body,' let us see that—tastefully, of course."

"Sloppy is the first mistake. Actors show up in poor, dirty clothes. It's absolutely inappropriate," insisted Greco. "Dress for the part. If you're a mommy, don't come in wearing shorts and a low-cut tank top. You shouldn't leave it up to the imagination of the [casting director] to recreate your proper attire. Talent being equal, we will choose the actor who looks closest to the part."

According to Barry, the big mistake is lying about your looks. "Come on folks, if you're unattractive, *be* unattractive. Do you think Steve Buscemi had 'glam' shots done? Be yourself!" Another mistake cited by Barry is bad makeup. "You may think you know what you're doing, but have someone help you. I've seen fake eyelashes, overabundance of eyeliner, and badly-applied lipstick too many times."

Another casting director who values the honest presentation of an actor's self is Cobe-Ross. "Sometimes looking real is more important than looking hot or sexy. For my last two PBS series, actors lost jobs because they looked like actors and not real people."

Lind commented that a too-contemporary look is a mistake. "Women pluck their eyebrows and draw them in. That doesn't work for period pieces." Period piece or not, one casting director insisted that the primary mistakes she sees are, "Tattoos and piercings. Unless they intend to make a career of those kind of parts—bikers, thugs—that's a mistake."

Another issue is *not having* a specific look. "No originality," said Smyles, is the first mistake actors make. Marki Costello, who specializes in host casting, agreed. "The biggest mistake actors make when it comes to their look is not having one. Create one," she advised.

The Importance of a *Look*

"It's extremely important," Tondino insisted. "Quite often, the best actor doesn't win out because they just don't have the right look. Sadly, a lot of not-so-good actors get jobs just because they look right."

"Yes! This is a profession. You should behave, dress, and present yourself in all ways as a person proud and happy about your choices and accomplishments in this profession. If you are in an audition, someone called you to be here. Be happy to be working—and auditioning *is* working—in the profession of your choice," Greco advised.

"Like it or not, the look is very important. If a casting director is looking for a woman who has endured a hard life in 1885 Montana and you show up looking like Grace Kelly all coiffed and beautiful, this is going to make it difficult for us," Alderman stressed.

Linda Phillips-Palo, CSA, who has cast a string of features for Francis Ford Coppola, agreed that the look is important, but noted that the actor is who she wants to see. "The most important thing is to come in ready to read for the character. Please don't be in character when you arrive. When I cast, I like to let the personality of the actor bleed through into the character. That shows me more than anything if the actor is right. I like the actors to show their stuff."

"Look is important to the part," Costello insisted. "Why not make it easier on the casting director by conveying the look when you walk in to read?" Snyder went so far as to quantify the importance. "I was told a long time ago that 90% of casting is what you look like and what your photo looks like. The other 10% is that we pray you can act and take direction. I hate to say it, but the initial casting choices are based on a type that comes from the storyline."

"Sometimes, yes, but skill also plays an important factor. A look can be enhanced—even fabricated—but skill cannot," said Smyles.

"Yes, but I can name two stars that walked into my office before they were stars and their special talents overcame the fact that they didn't exactly have the look that the producers insisted upon," recalled Paladini. "The casting director's job is to have a sense for when we can push the envelope."

"The best of us," Arsenault explained, "know we can be dazzled by fresh talent, inspired by a unique reading, and know magic when we see it happening."

"An actor's own uniqueness is his most important asset. What's important to remember," Ladki continued, "is that that largely comes from within and has little to do with exteriors. Yes, actors should be concerned with their looks. It's part of their job. They should keep an attractive weight unless they only want to be considered for [character] roles. They should be well-groomed and smell good. That's important when going in for any job interview—which is what an audition is."

Reinvention

Stalling out between jobs is not an uncommon experience in Hollywood. What's an actor to do? One option is reinvention. I'm a really big fan of the style and class Michael Chiklis showed in reinventing himself as an actor.

He really made a choice to change the course of his career. Chiklis had done *The Commish* and then the oh-so-bad sitcom *Daddio*. He was overweight, balding beyond help, and always playing the lovable goofball roles—far outside of what his actual age range *should* have been. After *Daddio* was cancelled, he found *no* work because he really wanted to start playing roles his own age.

He got depressed with the options available to him, having convinced the industry he could only play "that type." Still, he kept trying, kept looking for other options, and then had a heart-to-heart with his wife about their options, should he consider not accepting further goofball roles.

His wife sat him down and explained that she would be by his side no matter how tight money got, while he reinvented himself. They put a plan of action into place: weight-loss regimen, lifting weights and training every day, working with scripts he had never been considered for previously, and shaving his head. Then, in a serendipitous trip to Gymboree to pick up their child, Chiklis and his wife met the creator of FX's edgy series *The Shield.*

While Chiklis refers to the dark, dry spell of his career as a crossroads, he also knows that it took getting to that level of depression to enable him to make such a major change in himself and book a role in the groundbreaking cop drama. Here he had been desperate to have an impact come from his work as an actor. A year later, Chiklis was thanking Emmy voters.

This is an awesome story about the importance of taking control of your career when it has stalled out in this town. It's inspirational and something that couldn't happen to a nicer guy.

Commitment

Actors have to juggle a freelance schedule. You may say yes to a role that keeps you from accepting another. Or, you may choose to break your first commitment in order to take the later-offered role. What's my take on that? It's better business to state your availability up front and honor your commitments. It's okay to *not* be available—but to say that you are and then renege on that agreement is just not cool.

What if you've accepted extra work when suddenly a principal booking comes along? Well, first off—were I in that situation—I'd have told the extra bookers that I was available *only* if the principal booking didn't come through (of course, this is assuming I was aware that something for which I auditioned could still *happen*). That way, I wouldn't be canceling as much as letting them know that the booking I'd told them was a *maybe* had become a *yes*, therefore changing my commitment to them to a *no*.

I know it's hard to live like that for too long, so I'm certainly aware that it's just easier to make the plan and then, when something "bigger, better, wow," comes along, to accept *that* offer and risk spoiling the relationship with the people you cancel on.

However, in the grand scheme of things, it is important to remember that you are moving toward the goal of being a working actor. Attaining that goal requires years of healthy relationships. Keeping your word is a major way to accomplish that goal.

This is why many commercial casting directors put actors on "avail." When they get to their top three or four choices, they'll put each actor on avail in order to cover their bases. That means that you, as one of the actors on avail, shouldn't accept any other job that comes your way for those shoot dates without first stating that you will cancel, if the job for which you're on avail comes through.

It's hard for any party to hear that you're not going to keep a commitment to them (regardless of the timing or anything else). It's just business, and their frustration comes from having thought a role was filled and finding they still have work to do after all. Be prepared for a potentially frustrated reaction and find a way to deal with the other party's disappointment without taking any harsh words too personally.

Yes, actors do have to juggle a lot of various money-making endeavors in order to make ends meet between regular acting jobs. I think that's a large part of why an actor's life is a courageous existence. It requires so much faith in the dream, but that must be balanced with very practical issues about paying rent and making choices that further the dream—bringing it more into reality with each choice. No doubt, it's tough. But earning a reputation as a professional who keeps his word is a valuable thing.

I recall reading an interview with a TV actor in her twenties who began hating her high school role. To demonstrate her displeasure, she started showing up late to set and costing the production time and money while they waited for her. She was bragging about this behavior in her interview! Rather than being a professional and working through the term of her contract (a contract no one *forced* her to sign), she earned a healthy reputation as an unreliable brat. Funny... despite her talent, I haven't noticed her booking more than guest-starring roles since that season. Think the word got out?

Part Two: Prep

Training

Professional athletes train every day—even in the off-season. Professional performers must also train whenever they are not regularly working. The craft is built on muscle tone, so to speak. To keep your abilities sharp, you must continue to train, to explore new methodologies, and to improve your range through various classes. Of course, there are more types of training available to actors than I could begin to cover here, so instead of attempting to do so, I will recommend that you pick up the *Back Stage West* guide to schools and coaches, call around to do some comparison shopping, and always do a class audit—where you sit in on a current class without enrolling—before investing in regular classes.

Casting Directors Recommend Training

Casting directors see hundreds of actors each week. They see thousands of resumés. Is there any correlation between the training credits on a resumé and the strength of the performance the casting director will see in the room?

I asked casting directors in Los Angeles and New York to name the schools and coaches that—from their experiences—turn out the best actors. Here's what top casting directors had to say on the topic of training.

The Programs

Several casting directors believe there is no substitute for long-term, ongoing training for actors. "Local schools and coaches don't turn my head when I'm looking at an actor's resumé," said Dino Ladki (films, TV, TheCastList.com) of the comparison to league schools. "I look for the fairly traditional schools—Northwestern and Juilliard in particular."

"NYU is currently the best in my opinion," Geoffrey Johnson, CSA (films, TV, theatre), stated, "along with Yale and Juilliard. I am afraid most of my choices for the best acting schools are located on [the East] Coast."

Theatre casting director Julia Flores added a few West Coast schools to the mix, but concurred that long-term training really shows. "[Actors] get more of a balanced and thorough training program as opposed to just one person's thoughts and approach. The programs at Carnegie Mellon, NYU, UCLA, Cal Arts, and Pepperdine are so strong that even though I may not have met [particular graduates] before, I often bring them in directly for my clients," Flores revealed.

Other long-term programs recommended by several casting directors include American Conservatory Theatre, the University of Cincinnati, the Actor's Center, and H-B Studios in New York.

The Legends

According to Matthew Barry, CSA (*The Notebook*, *Freddy vs. Jason*, *Friday After Next*, *John Q*), "there hasn't really been an *impact* acting teacher since Roy London passed away. Most actors love their coaches, but that doesn't mean they're learning anything."

"When I studied with Uta Hagen for three years in New York," former actor Mark Paladini, CSA (films, TV), began, "I believed that—due to the rigorous audition process it took to get into the class—it would have an aura of importance on my resumé. Working in casting for 15 years, however, and seeing Miss Hagen's and Sanford Meisner's names on the resumés of many actors whose performances did not live up to their mentors' ideals, I've come to realize that the name of a teacher on a resumé guarantees nothing."

Indie film and music video casting director Stephen Snyder believes "the gurus are still strong," noting specifically the training of Larry Moss, Howard Fine, and Milton Katselas. The high opinion garnered by having these names on a resumé is shared by casting directors Ladki; Victoria Burrows (*The Lord of the Rings, Rudy: The Rudy Giuliani Story*); Melissa Martin, CCDA (commercials); Paul Weber, CSA (*Dead Like Me, She Spies*); and Billy DaMota, CSA (*The Employee of the Month, The Last Second Chance*, commercials).

The Coaches

As Weber noted, "It's all so subjective." That doesn't mean there aren't coaches whose influence is evident in the performances of the actors casting directors hire. "Anything you do as an actor to study is going to be beneficial in the room," Elizabeth Torres, CSA (films, TV), indicated.

"Coaches can be helpful, but they shouldn't do your thinking for you," Flores explained. "They should just give you the tools to help you find your own answers."

Barry went one step beyond that in expressing his take on coaches. "If actors would just trust themselves, their work would be more significant. A good coach who is smart will guide the actor through the scene but leave room for adjustment [in the room]," he said.

CSA casting director Arnold Mungioli (theatre) described training and the work of an actor as *process.* "Taking care of yourself as an actor—training and coaching on a consistent basis—is the best way to assure that when you are called upon to perform in an audition or performance you will be in peak form."

The coaches named most frequently by casting directors include Ivana Chubbuck, Harry Mastrogeorge, and Margie Haber. "Margie really gets actors to transition their techniques," Burrows said of the cold reading expert. "She knows timing," Barry added. "She has helped many a student prepare for the horrors of going to network."

Other coaches that top the list included Arthur Mendoza ("I've seen actors improve very quickly after studying with him," film casting director Dori Zuckerman, CSA, volunteered), Belita Moreno ("I've heard great things about her," film casting legend Debra Zane, CSA, mentioned), Cameron Thor for scene study ("Everyone I know who has studied with him says he's great," explained Torres), Marnie Cooper ("She is amazing for kids. Her kids blow me away," commercial casting director Stuart Stone, CCDA, said), and Janet Alhanti (who was cited as being "great for comedy" by film casting director Cathy Henderson, CSA, as well as by Zuckerman and Martin).

Casting director Lisa Fields (commercials, *Blind Horizon, Fearless*) recommended John Sudol, saying, "We book his actors all the time commercially and theatrically. We can always count on his actors making interesting choices." Film and TV casting director Lori Cobe-Ross, as well as Henderson and Zuckerman, recommended Piero Dusa. "He is a caring and smart teacher," Cobe-Ross said. "His students work hard and are very well-prepared."

Zuckerman recommended him "especially for brand new actors."

Improv/Comedy

Everyone likes to laugh. Casting directors look for comedic timing and an actor's ability to think quickly no matter what type of project they are casting. While the Groundlings ("they've always had a first-rate reputation," CSA film and theatre casting director Stuart Howard opined) tops most lists for strong comedic training, it is not alone on the list.

"I prefer Second City Los Angeles to the Groundlings on the basis that they seem to be more open with their students. The Groundlings has kind of lost some of its cache," Barry explained. Snyder described both the Groundlings and Second City Los Angeles as "good lock and load" training.

Zuckerman noted that, while training from the Groundlings is an "excellent credit on a resumé, Los Angeles TheatreSports is the best improv [training] for actors who write." ACME Improv Comedy training topped the list for casting directors DaMota, Henderson, and Martin.

Improv is important to your skills as an auditioner, no matter what segment of acting you're looking to specialize in. I trained with Los Angeles TheatreSports and studied with Tracy Burns, Tracy Connor, Brian Lohmann, Wayne Brady, and Forest Brakeman—all of whom are excellent improv instructors.

On Training in General

"I like talking to actors about their acting teachers," Paladini began. "I frequently ask actors about a single concept or aspect of their teachers' curriculum that opened creative doors for them."

Mungioli mentioned liking programs "geared toward the working professional, so that people who are already working actors can have a place to grow as artists."

A practical question about training came from Barry. "Do directors these days have the time or patience to deal with a Method actor? Some directors I've worked with won't hire [Method actors] on the basis that it's just 'too much work.' So, what are [actors] left with?" he asked.

The answer is vastly different depending on the person you ask. Without question, though, casting directors do respect solid training. As an actor, that means you must do your homework and connect to your process, whatever it may be.

As for workshops, there are a bunch of those. Casting directors and their assistants conduct workshops, and so do agents and managers. The best way to know whether any class or workshop is right for you is to audit first. Auditing is important because you can get a sense of the teacher's style and personality, plus know if the type of students he attracts are on your level. Just do your homework, keep learning from every possible source, and remember that opinions are just that, opinion—not fact. Research will pay off!

Resources

Okay, "resources" is a pretty general term—and I'm not going to attempt to discuss every conceivable resource available to actors in this chapter—but I would like you to consider this section the one that lists and describes some excellent actor resources (many of them available for no fee).

Breakdown Services

Breakdown Services puts out character breakdowns for each film, TV show, commercial, legit stage, student film and other type of project listed by casting directors, directors, and producers. Breakdown Services provides these Breakdowns to agents and managers for a monthly fee. Actors can visit the Actors Access area of Breakdown Services' website at breakdownservices.com/access.html and see limited listings there. Very recently, Breakdown Services has introduced Actors Access Electronic. This service allows actors to submit directly to casting directors using their free online tools.

Some casting directors do not list their projects in Actors Access because they want managers and agents to prescreen the actors who get submitted on these roles, rather than contending with actors who self-submit and may not be ready to read for a role at that level.

Showfax

Showfax is the leading resource for audition sides. When casting directors list projects and roles with Breakdown Services, they also provide audition sides (the sections of the script that will be used in the audition session). Actors can visit Showfax.com to download sides electronically or request them by fax for a per-page cost or annual membership fee.

In conjunction with Breakdown Services, Showfax is providing the means for actors to submit electronically directly to casting directors on specific projects. Actors must simply create a free login and password to make their headshots and resumés available in the Actors Access electronic system. This information is also linked with your listing in the *Academy Players Directory*.

Actors 101

Actors 101 is a new program brought to actors—for free—by Showfax. The Showfax staff has put together wonderful panels consisting of casting directors, acting coaches, and industry professionals willing to donate their time and expertise for various one-night-only events at Take One Film and Theatre Books in West Los Angeles and Theatre District at the CAST in Hollywood.

In fact, Take One Film and Theatre Books has regular free events in the back room of its store. I have hosted many casting director panels in this location. Make sure you get on the Take One mailing list, Actors 101 mailing list, and every other free mailing list you learn about. There are always many things going on in town—and you can learn a lot from attending these events. Stay up-to-date on the freebies. We try to list many of them at calsnet.net/cricketfeet.

Pirated Breakdowns

Why am I including a section on pirated Breakdowns? Well, during one Hollywood Happy Hour, I mentioned that Gary Marsh—owner of Breakdown Services—would be the next month's guest. An actor said to me, "Make sure you ask him if he knows actors get illegal Breakdowns!" So, sure enough, when I had Marsh up on the stage with me the following month, I asked him (tongue firmly in cheek) whether he knew about illegal Breakdowns. "Of course!" he said.

So, what do you—the actor who will undoubtedly be approached by someone trying to sell you pirated Breakdowns over the course of your career in Los Angeles—need to know? First off: receiving pirated Breakdowns is a crime. Breakdowns are copyrighted material and they are sold to legitimate agents and managers specifically because casting directors like having actors pre-screened prior to submission on specific roles. Marsh has told me that he would—of course—prefer to include actors among subscribers to Breakdown Services. That would increase his subscription base by thousands of people. Of course, it would also cause many casting directors to stop listing their Breakdowns with Marsh. They would simply contact agents directly to ask to see actors for particular roles. Casting directors already do plenty of this as it is, depending on how much time they have to cast a certain role.

How is it that you will be approached by someone selling pirated Breakdowns? The folks who sell these get actors' email addresses from their websites, off their resumés, and from forums on which actors commonly post.

These people also get actors' pager numbers—which actors only give out for acting purposes—from resumés discarded when mailed to agents, managers, or casting directors as well as by posing as producers, putting "fake" casting notices in *Back Stage West* just to try and get customers. Bottom line, these are people who want to make money off of actors by selling something that doesn't belong to them. And actors really only hurt themselves by submitting on specific listings from the Breakdowns.

Keep in mind, should you choose to receive and use pirated Breakdowns, that there are bogus listings created specifically to catch people who are getting them by illegitimate means. Additionally, Breakdown Services provides a master list of all legitimately-subscribing agents and managers to all casting directors. If you should happen to submit to a casting director who likes to check that list and turn people in, that would be bad.

Breakdowns' Roles vs. General Submissions

Actors have asked me why it is that they should not submit using pirated Breakdowns, yet they *should* submit to casting directors on a general submission basis. Here's the distinction between the two: when a specific role goes out in Breakdowns, submissions start coming in that morning via messenger from the big agencies. Another round comes in that afternoon from agencies with smaller messenger budgets (economy service guarantees same-day delivery, but not same-hour delivery, like the more expensive services).

The next morning, there will be an enormous stack in the mail, followed by even more in the afternoon mail. Every submission goes into a stack or a bin marked by that character name, as listed in the Breakdowns.

Once the casting director's assistant starts opening the *bulk* of the submissions (early ones will be opened right away, if possible), she will make the job easier by placing the submissions into priority stacks (A-list agents, B-list agents, agents and managers with whom the casting director has an ongoing relationship, companies whose names don't stand out, and envelopes with return addresses showing no identifying information—also known as *actor submissions*).

The casting director or associate casting director will go through the first stack and note which actors should get session appointments and the assistant will start making calls. By now, the agents and managers who have submitted actors are already on the phone, pitching their clients: "Did you get the submission?" "He's really perfect for the role."

The end of the day can come before they have even *reached* the fourth and fifth stacks, into which your role-specific submission has been placed, and by then the sessions are set for the next day.

General submissions are different from a role-specific submission which must be prioritized before opening, just due to the mad rush involved between the time the Breakdowns go out and sessions must take place. If you do a general mailing or a general drop-off, your headshot will be looked at when there is *time* and you will be asked to come in *if something comes up* for which you'd be right or *if the casting director does generals* between major specific casting assignments.

Bogus Listing Services

Many fly-by-night services crop up each year, simply re-posting the roles and projects listed in Breakdown Services and in *Back Stage West*. It isn't worth mentioning any of them by name, as they won't exist very long under any one company name. They get caught, they reorganize, and they crop up again with a different moniker.

There are many ways that these companies create a list of what's casting in town. Some get the info from *Back Stage West*, some use the Actors Access area of Breakdown Services' website, others subscribe to Breakdown Services legitimately (as agents or managers) and then resell the information. Obviously, none of these tactics for sharing casting information is legal, but that doesn't stop people from trying to make money off of actors with subscription offers like this—which combine listings from multiple legitimate sources.

There will always be little start-up companies that exist just to try and separate actors from their money. I am always reluctant to do business with anyone who, out-of-the-blue, solicits me for business—especially when there's no disclosure of how they got my contact information. Always be careful. Deal with people you know and trust, or people who run businesses whose services you need and seek out through reputable channels.

Production Charts

You should make a habit of checking the trades (*Daily Variety, Hollywood Reporter*, and *Back Stage West*) for their weekly listings of what is currently in production for film and television. These charts are also available via the online versions of these trades (all with various subscription rates and levels of access). If you're trying to get seen by certain casting directors, this is a good way to know who's casting what. Then, a little more research on your part should get you a submission address.

For the films that are in preparation or pre-production, you'll find casting directors are often not attached in the trade-paper listings. What you have to do in those cases is look up the credits of the director, principal producers, and executives involved on those films (on IMDB.com) and see who, in the past, has cast their films. For example: Ron Howard uses CSA members Jane Jenkins and Janet Hirshenson almost exclusively. If you see a Ron Howard film listed in the production charts in the earliest stages, chances are, Jenkins and Hirshenson will soon be tapped to cast. No telling whether an early submission will make an impact, but it sure can't hurt!

Academy Players Directory

Stay updated on the filing periods for the *Academy Players Directory*. Every casting director I have interviewed has commented to me that the best use of an actor's money is placement in the directory. It is the "yearbook," of sorts that these casting professionals use to find actors. The minimum status required is either representation (by an agent or manager of record) or membership in one performers' union. This is a great investment for a working actor and you should keep your listing updated every year. You may never know whether you are called into an office due to your listing there, but believe me: it is *the primary printed resource* casting directors use every single day. Call the *Academy Players Directory* office at 310.247.3058 or email players@oscars.org for more information.

Avoiding Scams

When I first started writing for *Back Stage West*, I was asked to do an undercover report on one of those "seminars" that advertises every week—and on nearly every page—in *Back Stage West*. The seminars supposedly teach actors everything they need to know about the business for the cost of a booklet and administrative costs. Well, after having done my undercover stint, I can safely say that you should save your money, if you were considering going to such a seminar.

Go into any situation, wherever it is hosted, with your intuition on high. There are many, many places where actors spend money to further their craft, and it is always a risk as to how much each workshop, event, or seminar is worth. If you ever have the feeling that you are not getting what you paid for, move on rather than trying to stay longer to see if it suddenly becomes worthwhile. It's usually pretty easy to tell in the first few moments whether or not something is right for you.

Never pay an agency or management group in which an "administrative fee" is required to get your headshot into their book, onto their website, or the like. Getting onto an agency's "house reel" should not come at any charge to you. They want you on their sample demo because your work could get them a commission. All of the costs involved in representation by legitimate agencies are covered by the commission the agent or manager receives upon the booking of your first job. Never pay up-front fees! Watch out for any group that wants you to pay up front, in cash, or without any prior audit or orientation so that you know what it is you're getting into. Another excellent piece of advice is to go online and check out the companies with which you plan to do business before handing over your hard-earned money. There are actor discussion forums all over the Internet that take pride in being able to help beginners and keep them from falling prey to common scams (see *Online Resources* at the end of this book). It's heartbreaking, because scammers manipulate your dreams in order to make a sale, but that's all the more reason to verify the legitimacy of any company offering to make you a star or improve you in ways that have nothing to do with craft or technique—all for the cost of some dollar amount that you *must* spend *right now* or else the offer is gone!

Reporting Scams

Sadly, when people are scammed, they become ashamed and are not likely to share their experiences for fear of how stupid they may look, having fallen for the scam to begin with. Please, if you are scammed, file a report with the Better Business Bureau and the state attorney's office, then be sure to write a letter to the editor of your local paper and the trade publications. There is no reason to think that your "one little voice" won't make a difference in closing down scam artists.

Headshot Requests

One of the things that happens once your headshot and resumé are "out there," is that you'll start getting requests for headshots and resumés from people supposedly working on projects—as well as requests for autographed photos (usually from some child who has suffered some debilitating tragedy). Here's what you need to know: I am not being overly-cynical. In fact, *every* request for an autographed headshot I have ever received from someone with a sad story has turned out to be from a collector of photos and autographs—intending to do nothing but sell my autographed headshot down the line when I am famous. It is a tiny investment for a scammer like this to send thousands of emails making such requests. And, if you should be one of the current working actors who goes on to be a celebrity, this guy is able to make a lot of money off of a headshot you autographed from early on in your career.

How do I know these requests have come from scam artists? Well, I do a lot of research. Whether an anonymous headshot request has come from a "hot new production company scouting for a major feature film" or a "badly injured child who has just one wish in life," I hop online and visit a website called ReverseAddress.com and look up that mailing address they've asked me to use.

Many times, the addresses come back registered not to huge production companies with dozens of executive suites or to residential areas of families with the same last name of the child who has requested my photo but instead to private mailbox services. Does that mean that anyone with a Post Office box or private mailbox is suspect? Of course not. But when you are solicited by someone and the story makes you even somewhat curious about its legitimacy, take those extra few moments to do a search on the source and then determine whether the request is one worth granting.

And, if you do supply the photo, don't be surprised to see your headshot for sale on eBay.com down the line!

Part Three: Materials

Headshots and Resumés

I've surveyed many casting directors about the importance of an actor's look in the casting process, and one of the things that *keeps* coming up is how important it is that an actor look *exactly* like his headshot. This really is the most important element of the headshot, and it is because of that fact that I am leading off this chapter with that absolute: if you do not look like your headshot, get new headshots. Period.

Color headshots are becoming more and more popular due to the drop in cost for digital photography. If you have red hair or extremely bright eyes or lovely skin that loses its glow in black-and-white, consider going forward with color headshots. They really do stand out and are still *just* uncommon enough that they aren't overdone. Yet.

Choosing a Photographer

Look at the most captivating headshots of actors you know—or the headshots you see posted on various websites—and find out who shot them. Are you consistently drawn to photos by the same photographer? Time to make an appointment to view that photographer's work more in-depth. Don't be seduced by the "celebrity photographs" anyone has taken. Those tend to be more like promotional photos than traditional headshots, and you will not shoot in conditions similar to those the celebrities encountered.

Make an appointment with several photographers whose work you like and determine whether you connect, personally and professionally. This is an investment in the most vital of your marketing tools. You must be sure the following questions are answered.

Does the photographer share your goals for the session? Does he agree with how you see yourself and how you hope to market yourself? Are you comfortable in his studio? How long is your photo session? Do you know whether you'll be shooting in-studio or outdoors, using natural light? How long will it take to get your proofsheets back? And how long after you have selected photos from that proofsheet will it take to get 4x6 prints? 8x10 prints? Do you own the copyright of the photos, once you've paid for them? Do you retain the negatives? Are you shooting digitally? Will these be color headshots? What is the cost for the session and does that include hair and makeup? What is the cost for the prints? Will the photographer help you choose the best shots and consult with you after the proofsheet is back?

Get all of these questions answered up front and weigh all of these factors from each of the photographers you meet before selecting a photographer and booking a session.

The Session Itself

Arrive early (and well-rested) so that you are not stressed or scattered. That sort of thing will certainly show up in your photos. Bring several clothing choices with you. You should've discussed options with the photographer at your initial meeting, so that you bring the proper colors, textures, and patterns (in general, go easy on the patterns). Make sure you bring clothing options that fit your *type* (see *What's My Type?*) and allow you to have a shot or two that really market each of the various characters you tend to play.

If you are having your hair and makeup done there, prior to the session itself, make sure you have brought your own styling tools and makeup, so that you are able to communicate what your "regular" look and colors are—and so that the makeup artist may use your materials if necessary. Unless the makeup artist is using a disposable wand for mascara application, you must insist on using your own.

If you are doing your own makeup, just make sure you've read up on makeup technique for black-and-white photography. It is quite different than the type of makeup application you do every day. And don't rely too heavily on that "I can just get the photo retouched later if I have a blemish or dark circles" idea. Remember, you are supposed to look exactly like your headshot. Retouching should be used *very* sparingly. I cannot stress that fact enough!

Say Cheese!

How can I explain the importance of *having something going on behind your eyes* in your photos? It's something photographers talk about, casting directors mention, stylists speak of. I don't know how to instruct anyone on having *that spark*, but it really does make an important difference in your photo. When a casting director goes through stacks and stacks of photographs, the headshots of those actors who look "dead in the eyes" will always get put aside (unless, of course, she's casting a zombie role).

Much of that spark comes from connecting with your photographer (which is why those early meetings are so important), feeling comfortable with the process, knowing you look your best, and being authentic to your type. Beyond that, show some teeth in your smiling shots (especially if you're getting some commercial headshots out of this session), take your time during the session, and have fun!

Changed Your Look?

What if you've changed your look—whether for personal reasons or for a role—since getting your current headshots done? If you've submitted your "old" headshot and gotten called in for an audition, make sure you say, "I need to let you know that I have dyed my hair for a role. I will be going back to the color in my headshot when we wrap, but I just wanted to be sure that you were aware I'll be coming in with a new look." No one wants to risk being told on the phone, "Oh, well, then don't come. We don't want to see you," but you have to trust me when I say that is a small risk compared to the risk that you will piss off the casting director if you just show up looking different. If you have an agent doing the scheduling for you, make sure that he is also representing you accurately during this time.

Be prepared that when you go in, you may have to remind the casting director about your current situation, as it's possible the assistant may not have told her, or she may have forgotten. Just get that factor out of the way and then get on with the audition.

What if you've simply cut your hair? If your headshot is close-in enough that your hair length isn't an issue, you could be okay using an older headshot that still looks like you. If, on the other hand, you have gained or lost weight, changed your hair significantly, or have matured in your looks (and now look different from your headshot), be prepared to get new ones. In general, you should get new headshots every two or three years.

Larger Headshots

In markets outside of Los Angeles, actors are sometimes using larger-format headshots (8.5x11 rather than 8x10). Casting directors in Los Angeles will actually toss out larger headshots—because they stick out in a stack and can't be as easily bound or banded while being transported or grouped for producers to see. Sounds silly, I know, but it does seem to be an issue for most people I've surveyed. So, while you may have been told that having a larger headshot will get you attention; know that it may be the type of attention that sends your extra-large headshot to the trash bin.

Issues That Matter Very Little

Actors always wonder whether a horizontal headshot is a nuisance to the casting director, or whether a headshot with borders is taken more seriously than one without, if they should stamp "redhead" on the photo if they have red hair. These issues, quite simply, are a matter of taste and nothing else. So, go with your preference and don't try to figure out what each and every casting director wants to see. The only thing that really matters, when it comes to headshots, is that you look exactly like them! Have I mentioned that enough?

Resumés Attached to Headshots

Getting the resumé onto the back of the headshot is one of the—comically so—most discussed topics among actors. First off: there is no one *right* way to do this. Read up on the options and do what you please. But whatever you do: attach the resumé to the headshot and make sure your name and contact information is on both, in case they get separated.

That said, I think printing your resumé directly onto the back of the headshot is a great idea. I think it's most cost effective to do so from your own laser printer. If you don't have a laser printer or don't care to put it through the rigorous task of putting hundreds of card-stock lithographs through its rollers, you should be able to get about 100 copies printed up at your local copy shop for around $20. Note: you generally cannot print directly on the back of a photographic print (vs. litho) of your headshot using a laser printer. The heat will melt the photographic paper and ruin both the headshot and the printer itself. Some people have found ink jet printing to be a good option for photographic paper headshots.

One thing to watch out for, in the printed-on version: if you're doing a lot of work and would need to update your resumé more quickly than you'd run out of the number you have printed up, you will find you're having to write in your new credits. If it's more than just one or two new things it could start to look sloppy. An option then is to print a new resumé on paper and staple it to the headshot, covering up the printed-on version of the resumé, if updates are coming that fast.

Many casting directors prefer printed-on resumés because, when printed on, credits and contact information cannot get separated from the headshot. I had no idea how frequently this must happen until I started interviewing casting directors. Apparently, glue dries up and resumés fall off, or staples get snagged and rip resumés off. Then, when the casting director wants to hire you, your contact information is nowhere in sight. Of course, you can combat this by printing your name, contact number, and/or agency logo on the front of your photo (in the border), or by writing in (or stamping) your contact information on the back of each photo, just to be safe.

If you decide to go with the non-printed-on version, make sure you trim your resumé to the size of the headshot! The easiest way to handle this is to set the margins in your word processing program to leave the most room on *two* sides, so that you're not trimming all four edges (major time-waster). Staple the resumé at the two top corners and once at the center bottom of the headshot, under your name. Voila!

What To List

If you are at the beginning of your film and TV career and don't have many credits, you'll still need a resumé. So, think about video work you may have done (Were you in a recruiting video for your college, perhaps?) and include student films. If you have none, then you'll lead off with your theatre credits and your training while you build the on-camera section of your resumé by volunteering to work for "copy, credit, meals" on student and independent projects. Even if the project never sees a screen outside of a classroom, your work in it is certainly worth putting on a resumé. Combine your Film and Television credits under one header until you have enough of each to split them up.

There is nothing wrong with being a beginner. Still, you'll do better admitting that rather than listing extra work or faking your credits. Worried that you're using credits that are a year or more "too old" for the resumé? There's no need to say when certain performances took place. Just list your biggest roles first, and separate training from professional productions on your resumé. You'll bump off older credits as you build current ones. Similarly, you will remove minor roles as major ones become more plentiful.

Don't put your home phone number on your resumé.

Depending on where you're sending those headshots, you never know where they will end up (dumpster, eBay, perhaps in the hands of a scam artist, a stalker). So, if you've submitted your headshot and resumé using an envelope that has your home address as the return address and then you've provided your home phone number (oh, and your photo, of course)... well, you see how this could be a dangerous combination.

Many actors get pagers or service numbers that are for nothing but acting. That way, any call that comes through on those lines has come from someone who has received your headshot and resumé. The costs vary on these services, but most are generally affordable and reliable and all are much safer to list than your home phone number. Just remember, if you have a pager, keep that sucker loaded with new batteries and always pay the bill on time! Casting directors can't reach you if they get a "temporarily out of service" message when they call.

Billing

In a feature film, you are a principal if you worked throughout the film. Lead, star, co-star—these terms are fine too, but "principal" is the industry standard. Whatever you do, do not spell "principal" "principle." I know casting directors who will toss resumés with that all-too-common error at first sight!

You are "supporting" if you have a few scenes in which you are doing more than delivering one line against a principal. Your role is "featured" if you are in one scene. Extra work—even featured extra work—does not belong on a resumé. Ever.

In television, your billing will match the language in your contract. The terminology will appear right there. Series regular, recurring, guest star, co-star, featured. Again, extra work doesn't go on your resumé. Ever.

Soap operas are slightly different, in terms of billing, than other television work. Recurring characters are in more than one episode (and are usually listed as "contract" players), principal characters appear only in one story line for one episode, and performers with one line (up to five lines) are billed as U5 (under-five). Yet again, extra work does not go on your resumé. Ever.

Theatre role *billing* generally is discarded in favor of the listing of character names. It is expected that most plays on a resumé will be known plays, so that the character size will be understood by anyone who views the resumé. However, if your production is an original staging or relatively new play, you may note whether you were the lead or a supporting character in parentheses following the character name. Also note—if it is an original play—that you originated the character. This is especially important once the play goes on to be popular and the role is being played by recognized actors.

Generally, you want to leave Staged Readings off your resumé. The main purpose for a staged reading, other than letting the writer or director see how it looks "on its feet" is to show it to finance folks to generate interest for funding (of a full production, film budget, and pilot presentations). So, hopefully, the main benefit to your resumé in doing a staged reading is that you did such a good job that you'll be asked to reprise your role when it's put up "for real."

Training and Special Skills

Should you list the class you're currently in? Yes, but you do want to be far enough along in the class that you feel you could talk about it, in depth, if asked about it when someone is looking at your resumé. Use the parenthetical notation "ongoing" or "currently" after the name of the class or the name of the instructor, so that if the person reviewing your resumé knows the person training you, she can chat with that person about your development in the class.

Should you note your college degree—even if it has no relevance to your acting career? I say that you should note your degree somewhere below all of your relevant theatre training (and perhaps list it in the Special Skills section, if it provided you with a somehow relatable special skill). Here's why: casting directors like to see that actors have a full life outside of acting. They like to know that you have lived a well-rounded existence and have spent time on the development of other areas of your world. So, don't list it because it shows anything relevant to the actor you are, but because it gives a little insight into who you are as a person.

One of my favorite sections of an actor's resumé is the Special Skills section. I've seen some really amazing things listed in this bottom-of-the-page area, and it always gives me an idea of the kind of person I'm seeing. Have fun with your special skills section, but don't get too cute. I have a friend who has "can tie cherry stem into a knot with tongue in under ten seconds" on his resumé. While many casting directors find that cute and interesting, others have told him, "Unless you're hoping for a porn career, leave that one off."

Just balance your Special Skills listings between personality-driven and actual, marketable skills. Include accents, language proficiencies, sports, vocal range, recreational activities you enjoy, and any licenses or certifications you have that could be applied to your acting (weapons training, lifeguarding, FCC license, horseback riding, CPR, black belt). You just never know what someone is looking for!

Demo Reels

One of an actor's most essential marketing tools is the demo reel. Yet no one element of the actor's marketing arsenal has so many variables as the demo reel. How long should it be? Can a theatrical reel include commercials? Should it include a montage? How can you get the footage promised to you? Does scene work produced just for the sake of a demo reel *count*? How much should you be prepared to spend on a demo reel? And, after all of that, will anyone really watch it?

A demo reel is basically a trailer for the feature that is *you*. As you make your decisions about content, length, and distribution, make sure you advertise yourself accurately and in such a way that leaves the viewer wanting more. It's all about making sure the viewer knows how to cast you. Make that clear, from start to finish.

Common Sense Tips About Demo Reels

Unsolicited demo reels are generally discouraged. Make contact with the producer, director, casting director, agent, or manager you are hoping will view your demo reel and *ask* whether it would be okay to drop off or mail in a demo reel. That way, when you do submit your tape, you may refer to it as "requested material" and thank the casting director in your letter for her interest in your tape.

When mailing a reel, package it securely so that it doesn't get too banged-up in transit and take it to the post office to ensure you've included enough postage. Enclose a self-addressed, stamped envelope (with the same amount of postage) for the reel's return. Industry execs who *do* accept unsolicited demo reels (and that's not the majority of them, by any means), prefer to receive reels with packaging for the tapes' safe return. If you can help them to get your reel back to you, they'll usually do so (and perhaps even share feedback. Some actors have enclosed comment cards just for that purpose).

Don't highlight someone else's performance in your reel. There are many tales of actors who have been cast from *other* actors' demo reels. Make sure, when selecting material to include, that you choose scenes in which your performance is the focus. If your partner's work is stellar and cannot be edited out without compromising the scene, make sure your partner is not someone of your *type* or category. Why should your reel put you out of a job?

Generally, commercials do not belong on a theatrical reel, but if a combination is the only way for you to fill two or three minutes on a reel, put your commercials together, after fading to black once your theatrical material is over. Do not try to "break up" your theatrical work with your commercials. That sort of transition is jarring and generally considered unprofessional by both commercial and theatrical casting directors and agents.

Lead off with your best material and include work that shows your range. Highlight your specialty and never use material more than two years old. Just like a headshot, your demo reel footage should be updated regularly.

What Editors Say About Demo Reels

Rob Ashe, with six years of demo reel editing to his credit, first began editing reels when he moved to Los Angeles after having worked extensively as an actor in Orlando. "In my first three meetings, people asked for my demo reel. I wasn't required to have tape in Orlando, so I knew I needed to know what tape *was*, first of all. I started going around town to see what I liked and what I didn't like. I picked up *Back Stage West* and called around to find out what services editors were providing. Then I figured out what I could do differently," Ashe chronicled.

With an eye for what would best serve the actor, Ashe developed a successful editing business. I asked him to break down the issues on the minds of actors hoping to develop their demo reels, starting with reel length. Ashe explained that filmmakers are far more patient when watching reels than agents or casting directors. "Your reel can be a little longer [than three minutes], if you're sending it out to directors," he said.

Other tips from Ashe include the following: "Open with your highest paid gig. If you have a scene with a *name* actor, include it, no matter what. If all you have are student films or DV work, keep the reel under three minutes, total."

As for what you should bring to your editor, in terms of raw material, preference seems to skew toward Beta SP-versions of the work (although footage can become grainy during transfer). Digibeta, while higher-priced, holds the best depth of color and lasts longer than other media. The half-inch VHS copy talent usually receives in "copy, credit, meals" arrangements is already a second-generation copy of the work. When that is edited onto a reel, it becomes third-generation. Dubbing takes it down to fourth, and so on. While it may take quite a bit of follow-up and persistence (and perhaps cost) to get a copy from the master, the final product will be far superior in quality.

What is the reel used for? Marketing. A demo reel is used primarily to showcase an actor's on-camera skills. According to Allen Fawcett, 13-year veteran demo reel producer (1,500 reels shot from scratch) and editor (with over 7,000 individual clients ranging from newbies to stars), "An actor needs a reel to prove he can do what he says he can do. In TV-land, a reel gets you an agent. There is no time for TV people to *cast* from a reel. In the film world, the reel is everything. Film people have more time to watch reels and more interest in seeing them."

Fawcett, who teaches on-camera technique and produces demo reels from his studio, describes being on-camera as "golden time. It is impossible to spend too much time in front of a camera doing dialogue and calibrating yourself to being inside of frame, hitting your mark, learning that you cannot do the things you'd do on stage when you're on camera. You'll learn that you blink excessively, lick your lips too much, things that make you say, 'Oh my God, I'm not watchable!' Those are things you should learn as early as possible, so you can begin to eradicate bad habits. A set is not a school. A set is somewhere that money is being burned by the second," Fawcett explained.

It is important, when producing a demo reel, to know your goals. Are you trying to land an agent or manager? Are you hoping to move up to another level in your career? Are you trying to get from co-star to lead? "If your goal is to get an agent," Ashe assessed, "student films are fine. Agents just want to see if you are castable." Fawcett concurred, adding: "Agents are looking at your reel asking, 'Could I have made any money off of this person in the past 30 days, based on what I've been seeing in the Breakdowns and what I'm seeing on this reel?' A reel shows your potential for booking, even if it's a reel made up of produced scenes. It's about risk assessment."

As for montages—those little clips of the actor in various roles, set to music and edited together in rapid succession—opinions vary widely. "Agents like montages. Casting directors hate them," opined Fawcett. "Agents can see right away if there's a conflict in their stable and can get rid of the tape after ten seconds. Montages are not as useful for casting directors and are seen as a waste of their time," he continued. In fact, some casting directors I have interviewed suggest placing a montage at the end of your reel, so that they can see your work first and your looks last. Ashe agreed that montages are a matter of taste, and his taste is pro-montage. "A lot of people say it's a no-no, but I feel that a ten-second montage psychologically gives people a second to sit down, breathe, get an emotional feel for what they're going to get. I like to put music down that matches the personality of the actor," Ashe explained.

So, how long should your demo reel be? My research shows actors have found success with reels as short as two minutes, and with reels as long as eight minutes. Industry preference tends to run in the three-to-five minute range. "I have never heard a casting director, a manager, or an agent say that a demo reel was too short," Fawcett commented. "Less is more."

And how much should demo reel editing run? "If you're doing a basic reel with your name and your scenes and you've come in with your tapes all cued up and ready to go, more than $80 for editing is a rip-off," Ashe insisted. "If I'm doing some major rearranging of clips and spending more than ten hours on it, editing will go into the $200 range. A redo—for adding a clip or taking one out—I'll do for $30."

As for fully-produced scenes from original scripts, with direction, lighting, sound, sets, props, and editing—

the type of full-service reel production Fawcett provides—the cost for four original scenes (40 to 50 seconds each) is $1,500. This includes consultation, instruction, and editing of the finished product.

Is there value to a demo reel comprised of produced scenes? "Tape is a marketing piece," Fawcett explained. "The main purpose of a reel is for people to know how to hire you, how you are cast," Ashe contributed. "Even if your reel is one [produced] scene and one student film, if it's great footage, it says, 'This is how I look, this is how I act, and this is how I am on camera.'"

What Casting Directors Say about Demo Reels

Some casting directors welcome unsolicited demo reels, others abhor them. It is important to do research before going to the expense of sending tapes out. For example, do *not* send an unsolicited demo reel to Big Ticket TV's Senior Vice President of Talent Development and Casting Donna Ekholdt, CSA. "It's like crashing an audition. It's an unscheduled appointment with me. Send your headshot and resumé with a request to send me tape. If I'm interested, I'll ask to see it," she said.

On the other end of the spectrum are feature film CSA casting directors Donald Paul Pemrick and Dean E. Fronk. "We'll put our feet up and watch a bunch of them at a time. But don't send a scene from acting class, or a performance at your sister's bat mitzvah. Include three to four scenes and tell me what show I'm about to see. Also, include some credits, especially the directors' names," Pemrick suggested. "If you've worked with someone I know, I'd like to ask them about your work." "It's a very small town," Fronk added. "We know those indie directors. And, if you want, send over a work-in-progress and let us tell you how to make it a better reel."

Casting directors who do *not* want to see unsolicited demo reels include indie film casting director Adrienne Stern (*On_Line, GirlsTown*); ABC hit *Alias* casting director April Webster, CSA; *Young & the Restless* casting exec Marnie Saitta; and award-winning feature casting director Debra Zane, CSA (*Catch Me If You Can, Traffic, American Beauty*). In fact, Zane commented, "An unsolicited tape is a little tricky, especially if it's not sent for a specific role. We're so busy looking at tapes we've requested and then editing together tapes of actors to send to directors and producers, there's just no time to look at an unsolicited demo. It's not a top priority," she explained.

Casting directors who specifically told me they welcome demo reels include Michael Donovan, CSA/CCDA (films, commercials, theatre); Patrick Baca, CSA (films, MOWs, pilots); and feature film casting partners Mike Fenton, CSA, and Allison Cowitt, CSA. Fenton underscored the importance of having a demo reel, noting that it must be made up of work you list on your resumé. "Don't go to a corner production house and have a demo tape made. You're just throwing money away," he said. His partner added, "If you have to include a commercial on your demo reel, that's better than nothing. Documentaries are fine. Industrials are okay. We need to see you on film," Cowitt summarized.

The head honchos at CBS and NBC enjoy watching actors' demo reels. Senior Vice President of Talent and Casting for CBS, Peter Golden, CSA, explained that a demo reel is more representative of what to expect from an actor. "I don't judge an actor on just their experience in the room [during a casting session]. That's such an uncomfortable setting for so many actors. That's why you *must* have tape. If you don't audition well, your most valuable tool becomes one great scene, even from a student film." NBC's Executive Vice President of Talent and Casting Marc Hirschfeld, CSA, agreed, adding a note about the importance of timing and variety. "I want nice, tight, short pieces that show the different things you can do, not three scenes of you being a hooker or a cop or a nurse," he requested.

CSA casting director-turned-director Ellie Kanner stressed the value of *good* tape. "You *must* have a demo reel," she insisted. "However, bad tape is worse than no tape. So, unless your tape is of broadcast quality, with good writing and talented actors playing with you, don't use it. Remember that the tape could be the last thing a producer sees on you," Kanner warned.

Tips for Happy Reeling

Work to get copies of your on-camera work. Build relationships with the people most likely to be able to provide copies *while* you're on the set. If you're working on a commercial, speak with a representative from the ad agency. Exchange business cards and make sure to stay in touch, asking for a copy of the spot even if it never airs. If you're working on a student film, perhaps get the name of the student filmmaker's professor. Many times, a request of the professor will aid your quest to get a copy of the student film, when your requests of the student filmmaker go ignored. With film, work with the production company. With episodic television, have a video service record the episode as it airs, if you haven't been able to get an advance copy of your footage. At the very least, set up your VCR or TiVo at best quality and acquire your tape on your own. Having copies of your work is your right as a performer.

Show up to your reel editing appointment with all of your tapes cued up and ready to go. Review the clips with the editor to make sure that you have a shared vision of the image you are trying to market with your reel. Plan the flow of the reel, from segment to segment, and decide on stylistic elements such as title cards and credits, music, and whether or not you will use a montage. Decide on the number of copies you will need, and if you need more than a few, you may find that it is more cost-effective to utilize a dubbing facility than your reel's editor for that facet of the process.

Make sure the material you use in your reel is *really* good (technically and artistically). Although we hope that agents, managers, and casting directors will *add* the impression your demo reel leaves on them to information they already have about you—from your stage performances, your resumé, and any prior auditions you've had with them—many times, the last impression you have on industry professionals is the only one they'll retain. Therefore, if you are providing a demo reel, it should be *at least* as impressive as your last encounter, if not far superior.

Finally, remember that everyone was a beginner at some point. Don't rush to get a demo reel together if what you need to be building up is your resumé.

Actor Websites

In general, casting directors are not very likely to go online to find actors. They have books and books of headshots in their offices and they pull these off the shelves far more frequently than they even turn on their computers.

Some casting directors do very specific searches online, but unless you have some highly unique talent, skill, or quality, chances are, you're a type that already exists in their books.

So, the question then becomes: "How do I get into their books?" First, get listed in the *Academy Players Directory* (which requires union affiliation or representation). Casting directors use these books to find actors every single day (see *Resources* for details on getting listed in the *Academy Players Directory*). If you're in the book, you're in their offices!

Another way to get into a casting director's files is to submit a headshot and resumé when the office is not slammed at pilot season or during casting for a major project. Is it possible that you are already in a casting director's files and books? Yes! Maybe you were in a great play, invited the casting director, and made sure that the box office was handing out killer press kits with your headshot and resumé inside. Casting directors do keep the headshots of actors whose work impressed them. You could have a fan and not even know it!

Having an Online Presence

Note that most casting directors who *do* use the Internet in their line of work do so to look up an actor's credits on IMDB.com, to look up an actor's representation on WhoRepresents.net, or to view an actor's entry at The Link (via SubmitLink.com after having spied the actor in the hard-copy form of the *Academy Players Directory*).

That being said, I have been hired from my web presence (on ActorsBone.com). A producer was looking for voiceover talent, and noticed my seven years of radio experience on my Actor's Bone page. He emailed me and asked me to come in for an interview. So, while it certainly can happen like that for you too, I think you'll hear of a strong web presence bringing an actor to a casting director's attention far more as the exception than as the rule.

Most casting directors work in offices that are temporary spaces set up for film production or they move from office to office, based on the project they're working on that day, that week, that month. That nomadic existence does not lend itself to online access. The casting directors who *do* work in one office every day (such as ones in studio spaces) have online access, but tend only to use it as outlined above.

Online casting is just not *there* yet, in terms of a way for casting directors to find talent. Of course, sometimes scouting happens that way, and it is certainly more and more likely to happen every day. LACasting.com has become wildly popular with commercial casting directors who *do* go online. Also, the new service from Breakdown Services—wherein an actor can self-submit on casting notices online—is sure to change the way everyone does business. Has it happened yet? Not entirely. Will it? Sure. It's just a matter of time. We still live in the town of Two-Martini Lunch dealmaking. That face-to-face interaction is not going anywhere.

Watch out for services that offer to include your headshot and resumé for a hefty fee—and that require further fees to maintain or update information—claiming that casting directors *constantly* utilize their site to seek talent. Rather than taking at face-value the testimonials you may read in their promotional literature, contact one of the actors currently using the service and ask whether the investment has been worth it. Make sure that the actor you consult isn't also—coincidentally—an employee of the online company. That happens to be an all-too-common hook.

What about services that offer actors the most cutting-edge information about currently-casting projects for a subscription fee? Here's the bottom line on most of those services: all of the information they claim to offer is typically available through existing services of long-standing reputation (production charts in *Daily Variety*, *Hollywood Reporter*, *Back Stage West*, Breakdown Services' Actors Access, Showfax). Use the reliable sources and save your money on the "services." Many of the "cutting-edge" services are gone within a year of starting up and your money is gone too.

A Website of Your Own

If you have an email account that comes with a certain amount of web space, you should certainly take advantage of that to get your headshot, resumé, and contact information online. You don't necessarily need to pay a designer to create your site. There are many tools and tips available to guide you through the web-design process, should you want to give it a go on your own.

My tips for a self-designed site: keep it clean. The less cluttered, easier-to-read, easier-to-access, and simpler-to-navigate the site, the better, as far as industry types go.

Provide a PDF downloadable version and basic HTML version of your resumé, in addition to a Word downloadable version, if you wish. Use thumbnails of your photos and then allow visitors to click on the photos they want to see enlarged.

Always assume that site visitors are using dial-up Internet access so that you don't overload them with entry page-loading media without giving them the option of clicking on a link to access such things as demo reels and VO clips.

If you don't already have web space with your email service and elect to use a free site provider, try to get a site from a service with no Pop Up ads or even Banner ads, if at all possible. If you compose your site yourself, I recommend staying away from Front Page, as it has bugs that disrupt smooth viewing for Mac users (which most members of the entertainment industry tend to be) as well as by some PC Netscape users. Outside of suggesting that you learn straight HTML and hard-code your page, I recommend Netscape 7's composer. It's easy to use and fairly intuitive. No matter what method you use, be sure to check every page you create in both Netscape and Internet Explorer on both Macs and PCs to make sure you have a page that works for the majority of all site visitors.

Know that your website will be more of a marketing tool than a "to be hired" place. If you're in the *Academy Players Directory* or on websites like LACasting.com or IMDB.com, make sure you link to those locations from your website. Also link to the sites of any independent filmmakers who have sites featuring trailers, clips, or stills from productions you've done.

If at all possible, register your domain name exactly as your name is listed with the unions (rather than something cutesy like your pet name), that way, when visitors aren't sure that a site exists for you, they can take a stab at it and hopefully find you with ease. Make sure, if you are listed on IMDB.com, you add your website to your information page, so people who find you by way of IMDB.com can click on the link to your official site.

Include a guestbook for feedback (use a form for comments or provide a link to your email address), agency representation information, instructions on how the site visitor may obtain a hard copy of your materials, and booking information. There should also be an "upcoming appearances" section, which you update frequently to feature your plays, showcases, film openings, and TV appearances.

Last, make sure you sign off every post on Internet forums, every email you send, and every cover letter you write with a link to your URL in order to get traffic headed to your site.

Submitting Electronically

It is certainly okay to submit a headshot and resumé via email, but out of respect for the recipient, you really should only send a *link* to your headshot and resumé, which should be located on your own website or somewhere else online. Sending an attachment is not only risky, it's presumptuous. You could be taking up a significant portion of a person's inbox with your attachment, and prevent other people's mail from arriving. Also, if users dial up to access the Internet, you could tie up phone lines for quite some time if the attachments are large. Besides, many people in the industry—especially at studios and networks—have filters enabled that send all attachments straight to the trash.

If the casting director desires a hard copy of your headshot and resumé, she can simply reply back, asking you to submit one by mail (and then you have the opportunity to write an amazing cover note, mentioning that this headshot comes at the casting director's request).

Monologues

It's not every audition in which you'll be asked to do a monologue, but because it happens often enough, I want to cover a few guidelines for happy presentation.

Editing a Monologue

Most auditors will expect you to have done some editing if you have to present a very short piece. There are plenty of two-minute monologues out there, so you may run up against less tolerance for editing, but even then, it is okay. If you do edit, make sure you maintain the essence of the piece, that it flows well, and that you've tried it out in front of an impartial audience of friends or classmates to be sure that the edited version makes sense and doesn't leave any elements unresolved.

Contrasting Monologues

When asked to present two monologues, you want to pick pieces that wouldn't be considered the same type. That means, for example, one comedic and one dramatic. Or one classic and one contemporary. Or one ballad and one up-tempo (oh, wait... that's for music). You get the idea.

If you're auditioning for something Shakespeare, you're going to do one Shakespearean monologue (say, one of the tragic ones) and then contrast that with one contemporary *comedic* monologue. That way, you show your command for the classic language of Shakespeare, your ability to do drama, the mastery of comedic timing, and— perhaps most importantly—the ability to quickly transition between the two pieces without compromising either.

You want to make the auditors forget the character of the first piece while you're doing the second one and you want both to be so memorable that the auditors are really left with something from your audition: "He has great range! Wow. I liked his take on that character. I've never seen that approach. I really went on that journey with him. Very solid, in all areas."

Pick pieces that show off strengths at the opposite ends of your range. If you're doing on-camera auditions, remember that subtle plays best. As always, connect with your characters beyond the journey of just the monologues and commit, commit, commit!

Creating an Original Monologue

Original monologues are tricky. You never want to do an original monologue when you are only asked to perform one piece. However, when you are asked to perform two monologues, you have a little wiggle room, using one established piece and the other, your original creation. Many times auditors want to see how you interpret a known character from a recognized piece. Choosing only original pieces would prevent that element from being assessed.

Another option is adaptation. I used to use a Suzanne Vega song as a monologue. It was titled "The Queen and the Soldier." It's a very story-like song with classic language and, whenever I used it, I always got a great response. But I never used it on its own; always as a contrasting monologue to a humorous contemporary piece from an existing play.

Choosing a Monologue

Certainly, you want to defer to professionals and peers in your acting classes as to what piece might be best for you. Definitely read the entire play or screenplay, when selecting a monologue, so that you have a comprehensive view of the character and this moment in his journey.

Choosing a character against type (or gender or age) can sometimes work to your advantage. Unless you're looking to do a monologue of a character who speaks extensively about what it's like to be a grandmother—and you're a man in his twenties—you should be okay. As long as you connect with the material and it's about something that could have legitimately happened to you, you have room to play around.

Remember—a monologue is a snapshot of a moment in a character's life. You are not portraying the character for an entire play, so there is room for creativity.

I always love the feeling I have when I finish a really good play. Like I want to thank the people in it for allowing me into their lives for a visit.
—Kathryn Johnston, SAG/AEA

Part Four: People

Agents and Managers

Before submitting your materials to agents and managers, you first need to do research to discern which representatives are the best match for you and your career. That means: get reading! For a comprehensive resource list, see *Recommended Reading* at the end of this book.

First and foremost, get a copy of Lawrence Parke's most current *The Agencies* guidebook. These guides come out fully-updated each month, with regular mid-month printings as well. While the information is extraordinarily up-to-date, judgment of quality of each agent listed is reserved for the reader. An excellent supplement to *The Agencies* is K Callan's *Los Angeles Agent Guide*, even though it is—by virtue of the fact that it is a published book and not a regularly-printed guide—out of date compared to *The Agencies*.

So, why do I recommend both? Well, if the agents you're looking up were profiled when Callan's latest book came out, there is going to be some very insightful information on their reputations and what others in the industry have had to say about them. There are so many direct quotes from agents that you get a really nice feel for who these people are and what their values may be. And with *The Agencies* as a guide to the most up-to-date contact information, you will have all your bases covered.

Of course, people move up, relocate, shift, retire, and re-enter the industry all the time. The nice thing about doing your homework with more than one source is that you can track where these folks have been and where they're going, while you learn a little bit about who they really are.

For manager-specific information, get Acting World Books' *Personal Managers* directory or the Breakdown Services *Agency Guide*, which also includes personal managers in its pages. Make sure to take notice of membership in the Talent Managers Association (TMA) or the National Conference of Personal Managers (NCOPM).

Another option for research on agents and managers comes from speaking with casting directors, producers, or directors you know. Ask who they go to when searching for talent like you. You want to make sure that you're not only matched with a good agency, but also one of "your level" and style.

Now, as for how to know which representative is the best match for you, make a list of actors you think you'd be competing against (either famous folks or performers whose resumés are most similar to yours) and check their names at WhoRepresents.net or by calling the SAG Actors To Locate line at 323.549.6737 to see who their agents are. If you search for actors online, actors whose resumés are posted on websites will usually include representation contact information.

Obviously, if you are the exact type as three actors represented by a certain agency, your submission may be off-target. Remember, the agents and managers—when seeking new talent—are always considering the holes in their current roster. Usually, they aren't eager to add *more* of the *exact* same type and age range.

After doing this research, you'll have a healthy list of agents and managers to target and then it's time to get going with the submissions. If you have friends who are represented by agents or managers you are targeting, you might choose to ask for a referral. Of course, they'll know you're considering their agent or manager, since you'll have already discussed this with them as part of your research on whether this representation is the best match for you.

A cover letter is appreciated and expected, but don't overload the page with details. Introduce yourself; explain what makes you think you're a good match for that agency and give a little information about classes you're taking (or plays you're in). If there are holes in your resumé or issues to discuss, address those factors right away. "My goal is to focus on adding on-camera work to my strong stage credits," for example. Make the reader a partner in your quest, and if he connects with that, you've reached the right agent. It's so important to mesh well with the person who will be "pitching" for you every day. This is a great first step toward creating that relationship. Most of all—when composing your letter—let your personality shine through. Make sure you provide all of your contact information, *proofread* the letter, and send it on its way.

When you've submitted your headshot, resumé, and demo reel to agents and managers and start getting calls to come in for meetings, you'll want to know—before you enter the room—whether this is an agent or manager with whom you would happily sign a contract, if given the opportunity. I know it seems silly to mention—since most actors in need of an agent or manager can't imagine *turning down* an offer or representation; but what if the agency only wants to sign you commercially or what if the manager refuses to work with the agent you're considering? What if no one sees you playing the roles your research shows are *made* for you?

In order to get very clear on these issues before the moment of decision is at hand, many people choose to post questions about agents and managers on Internet discussion forums. That sort of thing can provide mixed results. You'll find that most people in the industry are unlikely to publicly respond in the negative to specific agency questions on actors' post boards, since their public opinions may color how *they* are seen. That doesn't mean that you shouldn't ask for opinions in public. What it does mean, though, is that when you ask about a specific company and hear crickets chirping, you should take that as a sign that negative opinions may exist "out there." People are usually more than willing to share their great experiences in public.

Do you need both a manager and an agent? That depends. If your agency is small, you may already be getting "management services" from your agent. A manager typically helps shape your marketing plan and is much more hands-on than an agent at one of the larger firms. Agents can negotiate contracts on your behalf and often work hand-in-hand with managers to make sure you are on track with the comprehensive goals everyone has for you. After a while, you'll want a business manager or accountant to handle your financial affairs. Oh, and there's the need for a publicist once you reach a certain level. No one can tell you when the right time is to have more than one person representing you. That is up to you.

Timing for Targeting

During pilot season (loosely defined as the period of time from late January to mid-April—when actors are auditioning for and shooting pilots), agents and mangers are really focused on serving their current clients. A dedicated mailing to casting directors would be good during pilot season—as agents and managers just don't have time to consider new talent at this time. April is the go-ahead time for the agent search. By mid-July, agents and managers are set with their adjusted roster. They'll be moving forward with getting actors in front of casting directors for the many series shooting for the new Fall Season.

Another good time to seek representation—though it's a smaller window—is from late October to mid-December. Agents are then looking for fresh faces to present during pilot season. There will be little time to sign anyone in late December or early January, as vacations are at a premium from mid-December through the film festival rush in January. Once everyone is back to Los Angeles in late January, well, we're back into pilot season again.

No matter when you approach an agent or manager, stay professional and courteous. I find it is always best to be honest about where you are in the business (that you are SAG-eligible, that you are currently training to brush up your cold reading skills, that you have just wrapped an indie film, and so forth). Remember, you are assembling your *team*.

Commercial vs. Theatrical Representation

Some agencies are strictly commercial. Others (very few) are exclusively theatrical (film and episodic television). Most are full-service agencies, meaning they represent talent commercially and theatrically—and perhaps also represent writers, directors, and producers. What happens if you are offered representation in one department and not the other? What happens if you only want to sign with an agency commercially if they are willing to represent you "across the board," but that isn't the offer you've been given?

Start by realizing that the fact they called you in means

they do have interest in representing you, but that they may only see an immediate opportunity for you commercially. Decide whether it is worth signing only commercially and hoping they'll eventually sign you theatrically or if it is more important to stay available to an agency that wants you in both categories. If you choose to decline the offer, do still stay in touch with the agent with postcard updates, since their initial interest in you could pay off with a great relationship in the long term.

Should you sign commercially when you aren't offered across-the-board representation? I can only give you an example of what happened to a friend of mine who was represented commercially only at a full-service agency. He was tired of getting all his own TV and film work and having his commercial agent tell him there was just no way to get him sent out on theatrical jobs "at his level." And he had good credits!

So, he put together his two-look postcards (done litho by ABCpictures.com for about $100 per 1,000) and sent one to each feature film and TV episodic casting director in town, providing his commercial agent's contact information only. The agent started getting calls from theatrical casting directors, ready to see him for this role and that role. The agent called my buddy and said, "Well, you've got guts, going around me, but you got yourself some work and kept me in on it, so, I'll sign you across-the-board."

Boom! He's working more now than ever. Some might consider this a risky move. Certainly, his actions could have upset the agent, causing her to dump him commercially. But because people were ready to hire him and he was willing to have every bit of that work go through his agent for a commission, it all worked out for him.

Casting Office Internships

Many actors find that working in a casting office is not only a nice inroad to building relationships but also an amazing learning experience. The only way to really understand the hectic nature of a casting office is to spend time in one. There are several ways to do that—and some of these experiences have led actors to change careers (and go into casting).

Readers—Most casting directors are happy to employ good readers. A good reader is someone who has acting skills, but who has no interest (or no *perceived* interest) in booking a role through that casting director's office. A reader will know how to give and take and play off of and be played off of by other actors without ever outshining the auditioning actors.

Interns—Interns are most valuable to commercial casting facilities, which host sometimes as many as a dozen different casting directors per day. While many commercial casting directors hold permanent office space, so many hop around to various offices that a key intern will get the opportunity to work with many busy casting directors. Interns mostly sort mail, open envelopes, copy sides, and help actors sign in. They are generally not in the room during the sessions.

Assistants—Casting directors need assistants. These folks will do everything from covering phones to making copies to buying coffee to opening mail to operating cameras to reading with actors to analyzing contracts. The range is pretty broad. Assistants are often tomorrow's associate casting directors and next week's CSA members (okay, it doesn't happen that fast, but you get the idea).

Crossing the Line—Getting in good with any busy casting director is a good thing. While no one would advise you to become a reader, intern, or assistant with the goal of getting seen as an actor, most everyone (myself included) would recommend that you have one of those experiences— even if you just volunteer a week of your services to a casting director friend of yours. Being on the other side of the casting process will teach you so much that you can use in your own auditions. You will be pleased you had the experience.

Remember, though, once you secure one of these opportunities, that you are there as an intern. Do that job. Let your professionalism shine through and wait until your internship is over to assert yourself as an actor. Use this opportunity to learn and trust that—if the casting director really has exhausted all of her options—she absolutely will look to you as an actor. Don't push the timing on that.

Has it happened that a reader or intern or assistant just happened to be perfect for a role a casting director was casting and got pulled across the line? Sure. Does it happen often? Nope. And if you go in thinking it might happen, you're missing out on what is really the best part of working in a casting office: learning.

How should you approach a casting director about interning, reading, or assisting? If you have good relationships with casting directors, ask them to recommend you to other casting directors who may need in-office help. If you aren't "in" with many casting directors already, then send a non-acting resumé and cover letter to a casting director, announcing your intentions to help them. Leave out the fact that you're also an actor with an amazing resumé. That won't help you convince them you don't have ulterior motives.

Of course, the best way in is always through someone else who recommends you. So, check with anyone you know who works with casting directors to see how they got in. They may have a way to help you get in too.

Part Five:
Practice

Submissions

If you have an agent and a manager, defer to them about contacting casting directors directly. If you do not have representation, I would suggest that you send either a postcard or a headshot and resumé to the casting directors who are working on projects you feel you'd be good for—and do so regularly. If you send a headshot, make sure to include a short, but professional, cover letter introducing yourself.

Do not follow up with a phone call. Casting directors generally do not like receiving phone calls from actors, but most do enjoy receiving postcards following up on submissions, or alerting them to an upcoming performance (where they can see your work in theatre or on TV).

You want name and face recognition. You want casting directors to see that you're still in the business, year after year. You want them to see your progress. So many people drop out of this business after just a few months that regular submissions really can serve as a reminder that you haven't packed it in and left town.

Keep at it and you will see results. Don't expect too much too soon. Do submissions because they do pay off, eventually, not because you think one submission will be opened tomorrow, a call will be placed, and you'll be starring in the next big thing within a month. Certainly, that could happen—but that shouldn't be your reason for doing submissions. Casting directors are thrilled when an actor's submission comes across the desk at the exact moment they are struggling over how to cast a role (and you fit the bill). Face recognition. Name recognition. That's what you're going for, here. And, yes, you will get known as "that actor who keeps me updated." It can't hurt!

Go ahead and budget a certain amount of postage for submissions and always include a cover letter with your headshot and resumé. Consider it an investment.

That Dang Cover Letter

Make sure your cover letter is brief, professional, and proofed for accuracy. You want to say, "Hi. This is me. This is my headshot and resumé. This is my contact information. And this is why I think you should see me for a role on this show," and then you get to prove that you've done a little homework. Show the casting director that you know your type, the type the show uses, and where you'd fit (don't sell yourself as a star-billing type if you really would be best, at this point, doing a smaller, supporting role). Be respectful and grateful and then say that you'll stay in touch with postcards to update the casting director on your theatrical performances, agency changes, upcoming TV appearances, and that you'll do a new headshot and resumé mailing when you have updates to share. Include your URL if you have a website and close the letter.

I'm sure there are guides on how to write cover letters out there somewhere, but I think you should write from the heart—keeping it simple, of course—so that your personality comes through. Don't go too deep into your personal history. Just tease at the highlights.

I would think this goes without saying, but after

having interviewed a couple hundred casting directors, I realize this needs to be made abundantly clear: make sure you get the casting director's name right. Casting directors hate receiving mail that starts out: "Dear Casting Director." They feel it disrespects the role they have in the process when you don't address them directly. I can understand that. You'd hate to receive a letter from a casting director that said:

> *Dear Actor, You may be talented. I wouldn't know, since I didn't bother to do my homework on you, but just in case, I figured I'd make sure you knew how to reach me.*

Well, you get the idea.

What about stunts? Gimmicks? Silly little gifts and whatnot? Haven't casting directors seen it all by now? Yes, they've seen everything. Some casting directors get tired of seeing *everything* and are happy when a straight, professional cover letter comes through. Some become bored seeing straight, professional cover letters and are thrilled by a little humor. But generally, stunts are not a good idea. Sure, you'll hear the story about the casting director who received a roll of toilet paper with an actor's credits written all through it. You'll hear the story of the actor who sent a life-sized cardboard cutout of himself to a casting director. Actors get drawn in by these wild ideas and decide to try them and they forget the punchline. Stunts don't work!

I've heard so many stories about crazy things actors have tried to be "different." It's just amazing! And most casting directors pretty much feel the same way one exec described to me in an interview: "Sure, we remember these people... as freaks."

Special paper, custom letterhead, or some slightly unique kind of presentation can be fun, but remember that professionalism is key. Go that way, and you can't go wrong!

Segmenting Submissions

Submissions to the hundreds of casting directors working on thousands of projects each year can be overwhelming when you think about it as one big assignment. Here's how to conquer the monumental task by turning it into a bunch of smaller ones. First rule of submissions: don't do them all at once.

Decide what you want to tackle first: submissions to commercial casting directors, film casting directors, or casting directors who are currently casting TV episodes. Once you've decided which segment to do first—for example, let's say TV casting directors—pick the top twenty shows that you want to target. Make that list by looking at the shows (or their descriptions in the trades, if they are pilots that aren't on the air yet) and seeing your type already in action.

Next week, do the same thing for film casting directors. Target the casting directors who are casting projects now or who repeatedly cast projects for directors with whom you want to work. Again, do some homework (by consulting IMDB.com, Showfax, and the production charts in *Daily Variety, Hollywood Reporter*, and *Back Stage West*), prove that you are up-to-date on what projects they're casting, and state that you want to get on the casting director's radar screen for upcoming projects.

The following week, do the commercial casting director mailing (as you'll learn in *Drop-offs*, next chapter, I recommend weekly commercial drop-offs rather than mailings, but if you want to use the mail for these, that's fine, too). The good news with commercial casting director submissions is that you don't need to do as much research in finding out the types of actors the casting directors use, nor investigate which clients they're working with at the present time. Therefore, you don't need to pace yourself with only twenty mailings a week. If you're mailing, go ahead and hit them all. Just introduce yourself, mention that you know commercial casting is fast-paced and something that requires casting directors to know who's "out there" and that you just want to be on their list. Obviously, by the time you researched what national campaign a casting director is casting that week, the spot would've been booked before your submission arrives. So, use your energy wisely.

Overall, the reasons I suggest the segmented mailing approach are for your own sanity (it's not so overwhelming this way), for economy (mailings aren't cheap), to allow you to have time to do homework before each mailing (this really impresses the casting directors), and to keep you active each week for the long haul (it's great for the ego when you always have something going out the door to casting directors). It can be really exhausting to hit hundreds of casting directors with a mailing in one week and then sit around for the next three weeks wondering why you're not hearing back from anyone. Don't allow yourself the time to wonder about hearing back. Just keep the process rolling and you'll always be actively researching and submitting—that is great energy to have!

Should you ask for a meeting, in your cover letter? If the casting director is actively casting a project, she probably won't have time to hold generals. However, if you are doing mailings to theatre casting directors (many more people to cover in New York than Los Angeles), you'll want to time your submission to their season's production schedule. If you are trying to get on their radar without regard for what's on tap for the season (or if it's a casting director who works for multiple theatres), by all means do ask for a general audition. Theatre casting directors are much more likely to bring actors in during their "down time" than casting directors in film and TV. Commercial casting directors have no down time—or so they tell me.

When It's Too Late

Generally, casting directors are finished casting by the time the first day of shooting begins on a feature film. However, there are always last-minute needs: recasts, location casting, and delays in production causing committed actors to have to drop out. Casting directors sometimes stay on the clock, so to speak, for the duration of filming "just in case." Still, once the shoot is up and running, the chances that the casting director is opening submissions for that project are slim. More likely, she is opening submissions for her next project.

Of course, if you're in the groove with the regular submission schedule outlined above, it's not ever really about getting your headshot and resumé in front of a casting director on a deadline. You're simply staying in front of her, period.

Creating a Ritual

When I first moved to Los Angeles, a group of us used to get together every week. One of us would buy that week's *Back Stage West*, one of us would buy envelopes, one of us would buy stamps, and the other would take care of food and drinks. We would rotate the duties every week so that expenses evened out. For a few hours, we would sit together, decide on which projects to submit, address envelopes (saving on postage by submitting as a group), put Post-It Notes on our headshots, identifying our targeted roles, and get all of our submissions ready to go—while making a social event out of it.

At first, I worried that casting directors might not like getting submissions from a group of people in one envelope. Really, today it amazes me the things I thought *mattered*(back when I was acting) to people just looking to cast their projects. I quickly learned that nobody cares where the submission comes from, how many headshots are sent together, or whether the Post-It Notes matched one another! Point is: the most valuable part of our weekly gathering was that it embedded a ritual in us all.

Just like you wouldn't talk yourself out of brushing your teeth or exercising regularly, you find that doing regular submissions becomes non-negotiable. It is part of your routine as an actor, and it is just as important as acting class, rehearsal, and research. Part of my research, in fact, revealed that it's not just the indie films and student projects in *Back Stage West* for which group submissions are considered appropriate.

When I interviewed commercial casting director Stuart Stone, CCDA, for *Back Stage West*, he talked about grouped mailings specifically, saying doing group mailings is a great idea to cut costs. The one caveat he extended was this: make sure you're submitting with other actors of your quality, your talent, your peer-group. That doesn't mean "your type." What it does mean is that you need to exert some measure of quality control, because if the headshot on top is a dud, the whole stack may get tossed out.

With theatrical submissions, keep in mind that other submissions will be coming in from managers and agents who submit a dozen actors at a time. There is no reason to think it's disrespectful to send multiple submissions in one envelope. Just make sure that your cover letter specifies who is to be considered for what role, and—if it's a general submission—note in your cover letter that you all hope to be called in, but you are not a "unit" of actors and should be evaluated as individuals. And yes, Post-It Notes are fine here too. Just keep it all professional.

Refining the Research

Make sure, with such an investment of doing targeted submissions, that you have the most current *CD Directory* from Breakdown Services. Their quarterly guide book is updated weekly, if you subscribe to the email updates. If you are doing regular submissions, this is an important part of that investment—one you can split with friends, if you're doing the group submissions outlined above. Casting directors move all the time, if they are going from production office to production office. Whatever source you use for current casting director addresses, don't rely on online address lists. My extensive research shows that they are woefully out-of-date.

I've always recommended that actors, anytime a casting director is interviewed, tear out that interview and create a binder. This is actually how my first book, *Casting Qs: A Collection of Casting Director Interviews* started! There is nothing better than reading what casting directors like and dislike prior to walking in that door! Clipping those interviews—wherever you find them—can separate you from many actors who may be just as talented but not nearly as resourceful. You should also make notes about casting directors you see interviewed on E! (in performers' *True Hollywood Stories*, for example). It's part of your job to keep up with these people.

Remember: talent, professionalism, preparedness, timing, and luck are all it takes!

Student Film Submissions

There are regularly-listed student films in *Back Stage West* and at Breakdown Services' Actors Access website. However, many of the schools with film programs have headshot binders in their main offices. I recommend that you send a headshot and resumé to each department, with a request to be placed in the current semester's binder. Student filmmakers with no time to spare go there to find actors quickly. Make sure you provide accurate contact information, and update their book each semester with a new submission.

Terminology that's unique to student films (both grad and undergrad) includes *sync-sound* (which means that you'll be recorded on audio at the same time as video or film) and *non-sync* (which means that your video or film performance will be set against audio recorded at a later time). There have been some really nice non-sync projects screened at AFI and USC, so don't shy away from those just because that technique isn't the mainstream. Those films come off more like "voiceover narration" projects, so, if you're the lead actor and also the narrator, that's a huge role. If you're just the lead actor, and someone else does the narration, it's more like a music video. But, if you're trying to get tape for a reel, non-sync is fine, if it's good work.

If this business kills me, it will be after everyone in it has my headshot.
—Miki Yamashita, SAG/AFTRA/AEA

Drop-offs

When is it appropriate to do an in-person drop-off of your headshot and resumé, rather than a mailed submission? I've found that commercial casting director drop-offs are the most effective drop-offs, mainly because you will get more bang for your proverbial buck by hitting the major commercial casting facilities. With one stop, you can drop off twenty headshots. Yes, you can do theatrical drop-offs too, but there can be problems gaining access to studio lots and private office buildings. So, let's begin with where drop-offs are easiest and most effective.

For reaching commercial casting directors, weekly drop-offs at the busiest casting facilities can be a very sound investment. Create a ritual and just do it. You will begin to see results eventually. With commercial drop-offs, you don't need a cover letter or even an envelope. You can just put a Post-It Note on each headshot you're dropping off, with some little, "Hey, keep me in mind!" type comment. Use this note to update casting directors when you've added something to your resumé or when you're doing a play they should come see.

There will be bins—each with a few or many headshots inside—at each of the major commercial casting facilities in which you can drop off your headshots. Keep in mind that commercial casting directors may get a call at 9am that they need to create an entire family by 4pm. Oh, and by the way, that "family" has to speak Russian. So, if your headshot and resumé is in their bin and you fit the bill, wow, you've made their day! Also, by doing drop-offs, you see other actors prepping for auditions (which is a great learning experience in and of itself), and, if you see your type auditioning, you may be asked to read on the spot. You just never know.

Make sure your contact information is all over your headshot and resumé (or postcard, if that's what you're dropping off). Receiving a photo with no contact information is a major pet peeve of commercial casting directors. They mention this issue quite a bit, when interviewed. I suppose actors leave off their resumés sometimes when doing commercial casting director drop-offs because they figure it's all about a look, not the credits. Submit both headshot *and* resumé—even for commercials. Credits and training do matter here too.

The major impact of doing weekly drop-offs is the proactive feeling it gives you, the familiarity it builds with the commercial casting facilities (so you won't feel "new" to the environment when there for an audition), and the visibility it gives you, in the eyes of the casting directors. If they know they can count on seeing you each week (and I don't mean you're stopping by for a visit, just that you come in regularly and they see you), they will recall you when some job comes up for which you'd be perfect. A casting director can say, "Oh, so-and-so who comes by every week, he would be good for this!" And, then you walk in to do your weekly drop-off. Tah dah!

Be dressed to impress in whatever the look for your *type* is. If you want to drop off photo postcards instead, that's okay, just make sure your credits are on the card, as well as contact information. Yes, postcards are best for follow-up after the casting director has had a chance to see your headshot and resumé, but you can also use them as drop-offs, if you want to break up the monotony of the same thing each week. This is especially true if you have more than one look (with different photos on the postcards) to show off.

Commercial casting directors in particular are so used to drop-offs, you don't have to worry about being in their way when you show up, especially if you are starting with the big, busy facilities. You likely won't even see a casting director on your first few visits. One may blaze by from one room to the next while you're there, but you won't know who's who for awhile. Melissa Martin, CCDA—a busy Los Angeles commercial casting director at Chelsea Studios—suggests a weekly drop-off to each of the big commercial casting facilities: Westside, Chelsea, On Your Mark, Big House, Fifth Street, Village, and Castaway. She acknowledges that there's no way she can keep all of the headshots that come in, but that, from week to week, she may be casting something and your headshot may just be the perfect match.

I don't know that it's statistically more likely for an actor to get called in for a commercial from drop-offs than for a TV show or film. Honestly, it's most likely for you to get called in for a role you're right for (I know, I know. Easy to say), wherever that role is. If you know your "type," have done research to learn who regularly casts your type, regularly get your stuff in front of those people, and stay on top of any leads you get, your chances are far better than those who just sit by hoping their agents are submitting them appropriately. Worried because you're non-union? Casting directors tell me over and over again, they do not care if you are non-union. If you are right for the part, they'll get you in the union. Period.

If it's not feasible for you to do drop-offs every week,

twice a month would be fine. If that's not feasible, once every three weeks would be acceptable. Monthly is also okay—just as long as you have a regular schedule for doing drop-offs. Just get that ritual going! Consider getting together with friends and creating a buddy system for doing drop-offs. This will save you money on gas and parking, plus make the ritual more fun for all of you. Just remember that the big benefit to doing these is "getting seen" while you do the drop-off. If you're only going in a few times a year, there is much less impact to each of your visits (and then you're pretty much only relying on faith that your headshot will be in a bin at the right time).

Some drop-off-for-pay services exist and that just seems like a silly option to me. Sure, you can pay someone else to drop off your headshots in a big stack with hundreds of other actors who have paid for this service, but the whole point is "being there." To illustrate that point further, I asked busy working actor Stephon Fuller to contribute a story about how doing drop-offs helped land him a substantial gig.

Living in Los Angeles, the Super Bowl of Entertainment, we are surrounded by a tremendous amount of all kinds of production. As an actor, it's highly unlikely you will get seen for every role you're right for, even if you have solid representation. There are too many projects and too many variables.

My method of minimizing what I miss out on is to get in my car and drive to the casting facilities and see for myself what is happening. I am extremely careful about doing this because the last thing I want to do is embarrass myself, upset my agents, or become a nuisance to the casting community. I have a lot of respect for the work they do. After so many years of being proactive in pursuing my career, I can sniff out an opportunity with stealth-like precision.

One day while returning home from a commercial audition, I decided to stop by one of the busy commercial casting facilities to drop off photos for a couple of close friends. My own drop-offs had been done a day earlier. I was crossing the street when I saw four Caucasian guys my age crossing in the distance, headed to the same facility. I figured—if they are seeing African-American guys for whatever those guys are going in for—I should get my photo in ASAP.

When I got closer, I saw that one of the guys was a friend of mine, Craig Welzbacher. He asked if I was going in for the same commercial audition that he was, and I told him that I wasn't. He explained that he was going in for a callback and had been told to bring three of his friends. Craig and I didn't know each other well enough that we had each others' numbers, but since I was there, I asked him if I could go in as part of his group. He obliged. We ended up being a group of six and we had a great audition. A couple of days later four of us were called back. Another really good audition. At that point the producer put us on avail. Several days later, three of us got the call that we had been booked. It was a Honda commercial for Japan only.

We filmed two on-camera spots in and around Los Angeles for an industrial, a print campaign, and the Internet. It had to be the hardest I have ever worked on a commercial and probably the most fun too. Most of the crew was from Japan and none of three different directors over the four days spoke any English. It's amazing how you can still communicate with others even though you may not speak their language.

Through it all, I had a sneaking feeling that I would get to go to Japan somehow, someway. Two months later the call came in and we were off to Tokyo, Japan, to shoot more spots for the same campaign. As I was on the jumbo *jet flying over the Pacific, I glanced at Craig and thought of the notion of having missed this wonderful opportunity. Here was a commercial that I was right for that I would have missed out on if I hadn't asked to join in during a drop-off! I have to assume that this sort of thing goes on more than we would like to know about. I have to help my agents help me. We have much more control over our destiny than we believe.*

—Contributed by Stephon Fuller, actor

Photo by John Ganun

Theatrical CD Drop-offs

Casting directors who work on studio lots are always tough to see. Studio security is tight, and it's just not easy to drop by or even get past the main gate. If you're on the lot for an audition and decide to take advantage of the access to do drop-offs, just be very cautious. You could be escorted off the lot for being in an area other than the one for which your pass grants you access.

Casting directors who work solo in independent offices are sometimes more receptive to drop-offs than we might think, but it only takes one attempted drop-off at an office that has a serious *no drop-offs* policy to show you why that might be a really bad idea.

My advice is to listen to actors who have been in town a while. Find out where they've had successful drop-offs and where they've run into roadblocks. In fact, you may ask someone who is very successful with drop-offs if you could tag along one week, just to learn the ropes. That actor may enjoy the company and could find the mentoring aspect of the relationship very rewarding. Of course, then you need to offer the same service to a newbie some day. That's just good karma!

Getting Around

There is such complexity in the issue of navigating Los Angeles—and you certainly will do that quite a bit as you hit all of your drop-off locations and audition sessions— that I asked a busy performer, Robin Gwynne, and an independent casting director, Steve Lockhart, to contribute the following section on getting around.

The riddle of the Sphinx and the mysteries of the Great Pyramid of Cheops pale in comparison to trying to decipher the "logic" of driving in Los Angeles and it's been that way for a long time. The first freeway in the nation was a 6-mile stretch of what is now The 110 Pasadena Freeway, built in 1940. Not surprisingly, this city also has the dubious honor of being the home of the very first gas station in the country, which opened in 1912. And while we're on the subject of history: among the oldest human remains ever found in North America were those of Los Angeles Man. He died in the area of West Los Angeles about 25,000 years ago, perhaps from boredom while stuck in a prehistoric traffic jam (though some might argue it was while waiting for a callback or a call from his agent).
Just the size of this city makes driving in it

*intimidating! There are over 160 miles of complex freeway systems and over 5,400 miles of other roadways. The longest of these is Sepulveda Blvd., which within city limits alone runs for 31 **miles** (and yes, it gets its name from the extremely rich and powerful ranch family Sepulveda, the great great grands of Warner Bros. Television's Vice President of Casting Tony Sepulveda, CSA. And by the way, the accent is on the "u" as in "**pull**" and the other syllables are throwaways. Newbies to this town are instantly recognizable when they say "SepulvEEda").*

The shortest road, by the way, is Powers Street, located downtown. It extends a mere 13 feet (but since "Nobody Walks in L.A.," no doubt people complain that they had to park "all the way down at the end of the block," even on Powers Street). In a recent DMV census, there were 1,840,982 vehicles registered in Los Angeles with over 24 million peak-hour motor vehicle trips. There are no statistics as to how many actors were made late to auditions on account of traffic, probably because that is the pat excuse even in the rare instance that it isn't true.

Los Angeles covers an area of 465 square miles. If its silhouette on a map were an inkblot test, one might say it resembled a stingray, or, if tilted on its side, a ray gun. A coincidence? Or does somebody up there know something?

*To help add confusion to the already complicated equation, Los Angeles has whole cities inside of it, and some cities you **thought** were cities are not. They are only regional names to areas long ago swallowed up by Greater Los Angeles. The difference is not something that can be deciphered intuitively by examining the name of each "city" alone. You would probably have greater success studying tealeaves or the entrails of chickens. Beverly Hills is its own city; Bel-Air is not. West Hollywood is, but North Hollywood is not. Nor is Hollywood itself for that matter. Culver City is, but Studio City isn't. And Universal City* *isn't a city at all as it has no residents (though it does have its own fire department).*

The corner of First and Main Street is the center of the street and house-numbering system for the City of Los Angeles. **In theory**, *street numbers in the city are numbered according to how far they are from that downtown intersection;* **however**, *not all the cities within Los Angeles stick to this scheme, so numbers can jump around wildly when you cross city lines within Los Angeles. The same is true for street names. For example: if you are heading east on Magnolia in Los Angeles, it turns into West Magnolia once it reaches Burbank. Be really careful looking for an address on Robertson or La Cienega as they go through Beverly Hills. Not only do the numbers stop, change to new numbers for a few blocks and then switch back, but the two systems are very similar numerically, so you may think you're close enough to your destination to park and then find you are still a mile away. Are you getting a headache yet?*

Now into this mix add the craziest element of all: the people. Over three-and-a-half million of them within city limits. Their most peculiar habit seems to be rushing up on red lights. No one knows why. Perhaps it gives them more time at the stop so they can admire themselves lovingly in their rear-view mirrors and marvel at what a difference those Botox injections have made. Here's another peculiar behavior: they will often creep slowly into the intersection while the light is red, as if this action might save them a nanosecond of time. They forget that it is also Los Angeles quid pro quo to run red lights that used to be yellow. So if the last five seconds of a red light are considered pretty green and the first five seconds of the red light are seen as fairly yellow, you can see why our accident rates are sky-high. **However**, *when Los Angeles drivers are waiting to make a left turn, they don't creep into the* *intersection while the light is green, but instead only enter it once the light turns yellow, to the great annoyance of the drivers behind them also waiting to turn left. So, apparently green lights are also open to interpretation. This difficulty in making left turns in Los Angeles is exacerbated by the fact that the city has almost **no** left turn signal lights. Oh, and of course, no expensive cars seem to have working turn signals. Hmm? We happen to know a Porsche driver who says she never signals because if she does, people speed up to keep her from making her move. Noted.*

*So, **huge** city, multiple Cities within the City, and millions of insane drivers: great! But here are some helpful tips and caveats garnered at great personal expense, including bloodshed, to help you deal with this Byzantine system.*

"Rush hour" on weekdays is roughly 6am to 10am and 3pm to 7pm. Many freeways also have "rush hours," even on weekends, that seem to fit no discernable time pattern. Think: get to work, lunch hour, leave work, run errands, out for dinner, out to a club or movie, home late. So, what's that? Like, seven rush hours a day? That's about right. And that's not including the traffic composed of people trying to miss rush hour.

It's true: Los Angeles drivers do not know how to drive in the rain. Give plenty of room and move slowly. When possible, stay home.

A Los Angeles freeway exit will not always necessarily have an equal and opposite on-ramp. This can be very frustrating if you take the wrong exit. So, don't. Especially at night. A bad one is this sudden left lane "Exit Only" into the north side of downtown off the old part of The 110 South as it curves right. It sneaks up on you if you're in the left lane, and you might end up on a scary dead-end street with only your emergency brake to turn you around and no way back onto the freeway. Pay attention.

Here's a tip few seem to know: if you're on the freeway, driving along in one of the right hand lanes, and the white dashed line on your left gets thicker, either a double dashed line or a solid line, you're now in an "Exit Only" lane. If you don't intend to exit, this is the early clue to merge left. Los Angeles signs don't allow a lot of time for these decisions, but if you know this little "tell," you'll avoid many a last minute, hair-raising merge that no one seems to want to let you make.

Completely unsubstantiated observation: the middle lane (or the lane just right of the fast lane) on Los Angeles freeways tends to be the best one, averaging fewer stalled cars (they like to pull over one way or the other), fewer last-minute merges, and more in-it-for-the-long-haul drivers, or so it would seem.

*Some alternate routes one can take instead of the freeway: Sepulveda Blvd. between The Valley and The Westside and to LAX; Coldwater Canyon Drive between the Valley and Beverly Hills/West Hollywood (Coldwater is Beverly Drive in Beverly Hills, a north/south street **not** to be confused with east/west-running Beverly Blvd.); and Laurel Canyon Blvd. between The Valley and Hollywood (Laurel Canyon is Crescent Heights in Beverly Hills). Investigate Beverly Glen as another sneak-across to get over the "hill" (they're technically the Santa Monica Mountains, but **puhleez**!). Other alternate routes are La Cienega Blvd. between Hollywood/West Hollywood and LAX; Highland Ave. between Hollywood and North Hollywood (which goes to Barham, to get to Burbank, or Lankershim, which leads to NoHo); and Cahuenga Blvd., which is a great Hollywood to Burbank fly-through, too.*

Streets aren't straight in Los Angeles. Notice that there is no true grid. This can take you totally out of your way, or you can use it to your advantage. Watch out for

San Vicente Blvd., truly the Bermuda Triangle of Los Angeles streets. It's great for a block here or there, or to sneak through Brentwood towards the sea (if you don't mind veering north), but unless you're a seasoned pro, a good rule of thumb is not to count on it for more than, say, three blocks. National Blvd. is a little-known, handy shortcut heading west (and north-ish) from Palms over to West Los Angeles, but it has lots of turns and detours, so get to know it when you're not in a hurry and can pay attention to the faded, not-so-conveniently-placed signs.

Wonder why Santa Monica Blvd. is north of Wilshire in Hollywood but south of Wilshire in Santa Monica? Because the two thoroughfares cross each other just east of downtown Beverly Hills. Venice Blvd. slants north when you're heading east from Venice (it's only a block south of Pico Blvd. at La Brea, as opposed to a couple miles south at Robertson). It can be a very convenient alternate route to Hollywood from Venice/West Los Angeles (via Culver City and then the La Brea/Highland trick). Olympic Blvd. is also a good east/west alternative, but not once you're east of Western, unless you want to swerve way south. Heading west, Culver Blvd., after it branches off from Venice Blvd., is a low-traffic, straight shot to Marina del Rey. And if you're coming from Beverly Hills, the little-known curvy road called Motor Ave. cuts straight from Fox Studios on Pico to Paramount Studios in Culver City on Washington Blvd., which goes straight to the beach! Of course, all of these recommendations work in reverse, too, with the caveats reversed as well. Huh?

Since left turn lanes at major intersections often don't have left turn arrows, they become so backed up during peak times that it is actually much faster and less frustrating to drive one block past that intersection and then turn (either left or right) and circle around that block. A great built-in U-turn is at the left from Venice to La Brea heading north. It's there for the police station. Very convenient!

If you are trying to find the nearest branch of a business (such as a bank), keep in mind that in a brochure or ad they will be often be listed according to the "pseudocity" they are in, instead of Los Angeles. If you use a Palm OS device, consider getting a subscription to Vindigo.

Auto insurance rates vary wildly, so you may want to factor that in when deciding where to live. For example: on average, auto insurance is twice as much in the Hollywood area as it is in the East Valley, which can work out to an added cost of $50 to $100 or more a month. Ouch!

When you buy tires, go somewhere that gives a lifetime warranty; they usually include rotations, too. For gas, get a Costco card and fill up there whenever you can; it's about ten cents cheaper per gallon (and food and stuff are cheaper too). And get AAA. It's inexpensive and can be a life-saver!

Grocery stores are overly busy on Sunday during the day and during evening rush hour (see above), but are relatively quiet on Saturday nights. Unless you're going to shop at the Farmer's Market, avoid Santa Monica's Third Street Promenade area on Tuesday and Saturday mornings if you can. Farmer's Market parking is nearly impossible. Of course, there is nowhere in Los Angeles to truly escape crazy traffic. There are cell phone-talking, organic-fruit loving, fellow-driver-hating, non-signaling, might-is-right, Namaste-a-minute-ago road-ragers everywhere. Gotta love it!

*Now, freeways! The 101 Freeway is a **diagonal** freeway. It runs northwest and southeast! So, if you see an onramp labeled 101 North, when someone told you to take The 101 West, it is the same thing. The freeway heads north in some sections and west in others, but takes a northwest diagonal trend in general. Same thing to note* *headed the other way; you may see a sign for The 101 South, when you want to head east... same thing. And The 134 West turns into The 101 West (North). If you want to get onto The 101 South from The 134 West, you have to exit where the sign says and then get back on at the appropriate onramp. Oh, and there is no exit for The 10 West off of The 101 South. You have to take The 110 South, which is not referred to as that; it is labeled The Harbor Freeway, and it connects to The 10 West. This can be a big time-waster and steering wheel-pounder until you figure it out! It works in reverse too (no, not by putting your car in reverse... you know what we mean!).*

Also, if anyone tells you that The 5 and The 405 are the same thing, don't believe them. This is only true(-ish) way north of Los Angeles, where it is completely useless info, since The 405 disappears. The 405 is far west of The 5. They run basically parallel, but far apart, until they meet somewhere around Pasadena or South of Santa Clarita. Try to avoid The 405, anyway... it's **always** *a parking lot! Coldwater Canyon and Laurel Canyon will save your life if you take the time to get to know them. Even Highland is way better! Cahuenga is a great little throughway, too. Handy tip: The 90 Freeway is a great way to hit The 405 from Mar Vista via La Cienega or from the Marina... and vice versa.*

Other freeway standouts: from The 5 South you can get on The 134 East, but not west. From The 101 South (East), you can't get on The 170, but you can if you're on The 101 North (West), but then you can't get on The 134. The 170 South connects to The 101 South (East), but not The 101 North (West), but you **can** *get on The 134.*

And our personal favorite: if you're taking The Hollywood Freeway (The 101 North-slash-West) out of downtown, you have to change freeways to The 170 North to **stay on** *The Hollywood Freeway, if you just stay on*

The 101 North instead, you are actually on The Ventura Freeway. And if you're traveling south (east) on The Ventura Freeway, you have to change from The 101 South (East) to The 134 East to stay on it, if you stay on The 101, you're on The Hollywood Freeway again. Got all that?

*If you were to fly over at low altitude and follow the actual **structural** freeway, The 5 South gets renamed as The 10 West, and The 101 South gets renamed as The 5 South... the net result is if you take either The 10 or The 5 in either direction through downtown, you're actually changing to a different freeway in the process to continue on that same freeway.*

Also: have you ever wondered why everything seems such a mess of merging freeways southeast of downtown? That's because none of the through freeways actually go through. It's a sleight-of-hand trick where they just renumbered the existing freeways, and they feed you "through" using merging off/on ramps.

In conclusion, get a Thomas Bros. Guide ***first thing** and get familiar with pages 533, 563, 593, 633, and 673 (and their neighboring pages, but that's the easiest way to remember it), and consult it before every new trip. Always have quarters in your car for meters—you don't want a ticket waiting on your parked car after your audition (though some say that's good luck). Always have headshots/ rezzies (stapled!) in your car. Always think twice before getting on The 405 Freeway (and get used to the "The" before freeway names). Always allow **way** too much time to get to meetings and to auditions and to **set**! A nice little freebie: see that yellow curb? That's a loading zone... but only until 6pm Monday through Saturday. Yup. After 6pm and all day Sunday, you may park in a loading zone with no fear of the meter maid! No ticket!*

Don't give in to road rage. That might be the casting director for your next audition that you're yelling at. Lock *your doors (you **have** seen the highly-televised chases, right? When the bad guy jumps out of his car and into the neighboring pickup or hatchback? Not good for the actor in a hurry. Though you would get on TV!).*

Try to primp only at red lights, not while in motion. If you must car-flirt, do so responsibly. Get an ear set for your cell phone and use voice activation to dial. Oh, and if you call 411 for information about Los Feliz, just forget your high school Spanish class right now. If you pronounce it correctly, they'll never understand you. Here in tinsel town it's either Loss (as in "moss") or Lohs (which is correct) Feeliss. Feel free to sing in your car; everyone here is used to it. Drive defensively, meaning: expect the worst and make room for the bastard. Be psychic. Breathe. Signal, for God's sake! And don't pass us in the right hand turn lane at an intersection. That's just rude.

—Contributed by casting director Steve Lockhart and
Robin Gwynne, SAG/AFTRA

Where To Live

A good way to start searching for your Los Angeles abode, if you don't want to do a lot of driving around, is by doing some research online. There are many apartment and housing guides online, and you can do a search by price, by amenities, by size. Try the catalogs and websites for Apartment Cities, Apartment Guide, Westside Rentals, and For Rent, for starters. If you have no idea what zip codes to even start with, I'd suggest checking out one of those services that profiles neighborhoods for marketing purposes or flipping through your *Thomas Bros. Guide.*

Another good resource is the "Welcome to Los Angeles" issue of *Back Stage West.* They publish one every six months, and include a little map and an explanation of each neighborhood, geared to the actors' needs.

The best way to get a place to live in Los Angeles is to drive around with a good buddy and a cell phone, going up and down the streets on which you want to live, looking for signs posted in windows saying "For Rent." Usually, by the time the best places are up for grabs for even a day, they're already spoken for. So, if you see something you like, call from the driveway and say you'd like to come in and look at the place. Have your checkbook handy, along with references, as most places won't hold a unit without a hefty deposit and some words in your favor from past employers or landlords.

Is it possible to find something not terribly expensive, centrally located, and available? Yes. Absolutely. But, you may have to hit town (perhaps bunk with a friend or find a temporary housing situation) before you can really refine your housing search. There's no amount of online research you can do that will compare with the experience of being here and seeing where you want to be.

Auditions

Scoring an audition is always reason to celebrate. Your hard work is paying off! Now what?

Of course, you want to be prepared with the copy (provided in advance at Showfax.com or waiting for you at the audition location). You also want to do a little research on the type of project this is. What is the tone? If it's possible to see a copy of the character breakdown that was created for your role, that would be ideal. You'll be able to learn a lot about the character that may not come across solely in the sides you've been provided for the audition. If this is a role in an existing series, set that VCR or TiVo and watch an episode or two (depending on how much time you have before your audition) and know the tone, the feel, the vibe of the environment in which these characters exist, from week to week.

Definitely remove stresses over which you have control: your outfit (make sure you've pre-selected what you'll wear, have it cleaned and pressed and ready to go long before the big day), your transportation (have plenty of gas in the car so that you don't have to stop on the way, have your route mapped out using Mapquest.com, Yahoo! Maps, or your *Thomas Bros. Guide*, and know what the parking situation is, at your destination), and your marketing kit (headshots and resumés, already assembled and trimmed, copies of your demo reel prepped and ready). If you leave for any audition having taken care of the elements that are in your control, you remove stresses, which makes your audition go more smoothly.

Arrive in plenty of time to get signed in and prepared for any last-minute changes that could exist, once you're at the office (new sides, sudden addition of a scene partner, request for five copies of your headshot and resumé for an entire committee of auditors). Use a little time to get "in the zone" while you're in the lobby and know, as you look over your sides one last time, that you are as prepared and relaxed as you can be. If you're the type who gets spooked by being around other actors in the waiting room, make sure you tell the assistant with whom you've signed in before you step out into the hall or outside to wait. You certainly don't want anyone to think you've bailed on your audition, just because you're at the water fountain!

If you are given direction after your first read, please don't try to figure out what the casting director *means* by having asked you to try something a little different. It could mean the casting director likes your look but wants to see you go in another direction with the material. It could mean that your read was "off" from what the casting director had in mind and you are being directed to do the material in the "standard" way. It could also mean that your work was perfect and the casting director wants to see how well you take direction—how well you can interpret and incorporate notes given to you on the fly.

These are all aspects of a casting director's job: to know the actor she is recommending to the director and producers. So, it is always a good idea to prepare your material in several different ways—as well as being ready to act "on your feet," if you are given direction during the audition. This is why improv skills are so vitally important.

Rather than focusing on whether it is a "good" or "bad" thing to receive direction during an audition, simply understand that it is a part of the process and that you are enjoying a happy experience: engaging in that process with a casting professional who likes you or your work enough to ask to see the material again!

Having a professional attitude really will put you above your competition. The casting director will remember you as someone who was easy to deal with, a pleasure to talk to, and—assuming you nail your read—a great candidate for this or some other project. As they say, "You're always auditioning for your *next* audition." So, make it count, then leave knowing you did your best, and let it go!

Letting It Go

One of my least favorite things that actors do, upon leaving the audition room, is recreate every moment in their minds over and over and over again, constantly reworking the audition, the scene, the reactions, the choices, the small talk, the *everything.* Okay, look, let me run a parallel that may prove, once and for all, how ridiculous this actor habit is.

Imagine you are a grocery-bagger at the local market. That's your job. You do a fine job and sometimes you do such a fine job consistently that you get a raise. Ooh, more good work! A bonus! Promotions! Until eventually you've become manager of the store and, later, the whole chain of stores. You put in your time, you did good work, and you lived a full life outside of your job each day.

As an actor, your *job* is getting auditions and auditioning. Every time you have an audition, you are putting in a day of work. You show up on time, prepared to do a good job, and, when you leave, you clock out and go home, living your life, trusting that your consistent good work will result in a raise (getting hired to act), a promotion (getting hired to act consistently), or a bonus (getting a long-standing contract to act consistently), until you "manage the store" (run your own production company, develop your own franchise, whatever your ultimate goal may be).

Now, if you leave every audition reworking all of the choices you made, that is just as if you—in the grocery-bagger analogy—leave work and spend the next five hours re-bagging every sack of groceries you bagged that shift. You take out and put back in all of the food and drinks, you reorganize the bags in the cart, you change the way you interact with the customers—all basically "mind taffy," as I like to call it. You are doing nothing but playing mind games with yourself, remaining attached to something that has already happened and over which you have no control: the work you just did. It's over. Go live your life.

And make it a *habit* of living your life, or else every time you show up to do your job, you will do nothing but second-guess each choice you make, doubt yourself, lose confidence, and end up getting fired. Yup. Keep overthinking the auditions you do and you'll stop being asked to come do them. Auditors bring in people they love to watch. Who wants to watch someone who has job anxiety? Casting directors like to watch people who love what they do and are elated to share in their joy. That's what success is about. Every time you are asked to audition, you are being told, "I agree. You are an actor!" And every callback is a message that you are castable. After that, it's just a matter of which way they decide to go.

Just like you wouldn't have an attachment over what shoppers do with their groceries when they get home from the market (What dish will they make? What salad dressing will they use? Did they open the pack of gum on the way home?), have no attachment to the outcome of your auditions. If you know you did good work, you've done your job. That's all that's up to you anyway.

Casting Directors' Favorite Auditions

Casting directors see thousands of actors each year. They watch actors transition in and out of character, make strong choices, and sometimes blow the whole thing, only to start again and nail it, big time. What is it that makes any one particular audition stand out? Well, it's not always the good stuff!

Tammara Billik, CSA casting director for the sitcoms *Ellen, Nikki, Unhappily Ever After,* and *Married... with Children,* cited a favorite audition from those *Married* days. "We were casting an episode set in Chippendale's, and we needed actors who looked the part," she began, noting that training was not a requirement for the actors auditioning for the dancer roles. One actor, in his audition, read aloud his scripted words as well as his stage directions.

Billik continued, "He was talking to Peggy Bundy and said, 'Yes, Mrs. Bundy, I do work here at Chippendale's. He turns to her and smiles.' I pulled the actor aside and said, 'Y'know, the stage directions are to be read silently.'" When the actor began again, he made an adjustment: he whispered those stage directions. "No one in the room would make eye contact because we knew we were going to burst out laughing," she recalled.

Similarly, Marc Hirschfeld, CSA, Executive Vice President of Talent and Casting for NBC, described an inappropriate choice made by a sweat suit-clad actor auditioning for the role of the high school gym teacher on *The Nanny.* Hirschfeld has seen his share of sitcom auditions, having cast hits like *Seinfeld, Third Rock from the Sun,* and *NewsRadio,* but this one stood out.

"It's okay to indicate with clothing, but you don't want

to [go so far as to] wear scrubs coming in for a doctor audition. Also, I totally discourage the use of props in an audition. I just think it's a crutch that people use when they haven't put a lot of energy into the character." So, for Hirschfeld, when the above-mentioned woman pulled a whistle out from a lanyard around her neck and began blowing it shrilly in a small room filled with people, he wasn't the only one who burst out in laughter.

"It was ear-shattering! But she felt like she got a response out of it, so she did it again and again, and every time [she blew the whistle] we were like, 'No! No!' Needless to say, she did not get the part, but it was one of the funniest and most tragic auditions I have ever been witness to," Hirschfeld summarized.

Of course, there are the excellent audition choices that stand out too. Jane Jenkins, CSA, who—along with partner and CSA member Janet Hirshenson—has cast the features *The Princess Bride*, *A Beautiful Mind*, *Ransom*, *Harry Potter*, and *Stand by Me*, just to name a few, recalls fondly her session with Vincent D'Onofrio. "I have vivid memories of Vincent's audition for *Mystic Pizza*," she began.

The sides called for the character to roll around on the floor with Lili Taylor's character in a heavy makeout scene, followed by an abrupt confrontation with her father. "Most actors felt the need to grope me, grab me, or roll around on the floor by themselves," Jenkins explained. "Vincent got down on one knee and did the whole scene as if it were his close up." This tactic impressed Jenkins, as she shares this successful audition choice whenever she speaks to actors at occasional seminars. "When you have one of those physically-demanding, complicated scenes that is impossible to do in an office, do your close-up," she advised.

Katy Wallin, CSA, who has cast the features *Finder's Fee*, *Trumpet of the Swan*, and *BASEketball*, was working with writer/director Trey Parker on the feature film *Orgazmo* when she encountered her most memorable auditioning actor. "At auditions, Trey was great," she began. "He was so open and receptive. During the chitchat, he asked actors a yes or no question, 'Can you fake an orgasm?'

"One actor he asked proceeded to fake one. For ten minutes! I was embarrassed for us all: the camera operator, the reader. An employee here had an ear to the door, trying to figure out what was going on. Trey thought it was great. He loved it. The actor was brave and he did a great job but he didn't get the part," Wallin concluded with a laugh.

CSA member Lisa Miller Katz, with credits such as *King of Queens*, *The Fresh Prince of Bel-Air*, *According to Jim*, and *Everybody Loves Raymond*, explained that she reads with auditioning actors, even in the producer sessions—and has had her most memorable audition experience in such a session. "I was on a movie of the week and it was about this man who was attacking this woman. The actor had said to me, 'Do you mind if I kind of *go* for you a little bit?' He had forewarned me.

"All the execs were all around and [the actor] actually pinned me to the wall. It was scary. It was inappropriate," Katz concluded, noting that the audition becomes less about the performance and more about physical contact in such situations. "A lot of people are very intense about their personal space and I think you really have to respect that. If your sense is that it might not be received okay, go with your instincts. Make a move toward someone, indicate, reach for their hand, but don't grab them. I'm all for confidence, but it's quite astonishing sometimes," Katz said with a laugh.

Ruth Lambert, CSA, former Director of Feature Animation Casting for Disney, fondly recalled the professionalism with which Dave Foley handled his audition for *A Bug's Life*. "Dave played Flick but he was originally called in for the part of the walking stick bug. The session was running way long," Lambert explained. As Foley waited patiently in the lobby, a celebrity came in. "I had to ask Dave if we could reschedule. He was so great. He said, 'Oh, yeah. I just saw [that person] walk in. It's fine, Ruth.'

"By the time Dave came back in, we'd already cast David Hyde Pierce as the walking stick bug," she said. Lambert had to negotiate in order to get Foley seen for Flick. "No one had thought of him for it. Once he came in, though, he had it. He was exactly the kind of person that they love to hang out with. Those Pixar people love to hang," she said. Therefore, Foley's willingness to come back in and his great attitude—as much as his talent itself—won him the role. "You don't want to work with someone that's nasty. Our process takes so long. For the actor it's two-and-a-half years, and so who wants to keep bringing someone in that you don't like?" Lambert asked.

Indie film casting director Wendy Weidman had a memorable experience casting *Blue Car* for first-time director Karen Moncrieff. "I found that Karen was going through the pictures with me and picking actors based on their looks," Weidman began. "From my experience, you can't just cast from a picture. You get [the actor] in the room and see their work. Luckily, Karen was very open and willing to try anything. I had had Agnes [Bruckner] audition for me in the past, so I was aware of her work and knew we needed to bring her in for Karen."

Moncrieff recalled Bruckner's audition as well, noting it was Weidman's persistence that paid off in casting. "Wendy showed me Agnes' picture and I didn't know her at all. I said no initially, just based on her picture. [It] made her look very glamorous and older. Luckily, Wendy didn't listen to me and brought [Agnes] in anyway. When [she] came in, she had an immediate connection to the material and was very emotionally accessible. That was really important to me."

Finally, Julia Flores, who has cast national theatre tours that have originated from theatres such as the Globe Theatre in San Diego and the Arizona Theatre Company, recalled an evolution evident in actor Krista Jackson, over the course of several auditions.

"Krista is an actress I auditioned and used in chorus all the time," Flores began. "About a year-and-a-half ago, she told me she wanted to do more than chorus roles. I told her that as long as she could back that up with the work, I would support that position." Jackson elevated her craft to such an extent that Flores was able to cast her in the title role of *Evita*. "She was really incredible. She made the commitment to see the decision through. She didn't just talk about it. She did a lot of really hard work. That's what I respect most in actors: hard work. The actors I hire work hard," Flores concluded, proudly.

An Average Day During Pilot Season

Pilot season is a totally different animal, as far as auditions go. You have to live it to believe it! Crista Flanagan is a talented actor, writer, and comic whose work I first became aware of during a stand-up showcase at The Comedy Union. I knew she would be perfect for the all-woman showcase *15 Minutes of FEM*. Not only was she fantastic in her one-woman show there, but she ended up winning the fourth *Best of FEM* contest! Her talent isn't just recognized by the likes of me. Crista has had a busy year. She very graciously supplied the following journal entry, depicting an average day during pilot season.

TUESDAY, MARCH 25th:
It's 7:05pm and my eyes are swollen from fatigue and exhaustion. I worked late last night and worked on my auditions for today when I got home. I had five auditions

today, and a job interview. I'm supposed to go see two shows tonight and then perform at The Improv, but I had to cancel my evening. I feel too poorly.

Five auditions... all for pilots. I guess things are coming to an end. This morning, I woke early so I could curl my hair. It looked terrible, so 20 minutes before I left, I got in the shower and washed it. I left with wet hair, packed my car with headshots and resumés, bottled water, and four different outfits for my auditions.

The first was at Fox at 8:30am. Since that means The 405, I left at 7am. Barely made it, but the casting directors were late, so it didn't matter. I changed in my car and headed back to Burbank. This one didn't feel good at all, but oh well. Grab some migraine medicine and change clothes in my tiny Toyota Tercel with the big scratch down the side. Put on pantyhose for this one. Yikes, it's starting to get really hot.

All right, moving on. Audition number three. Again, didn't quite feel right, but no time to think too hard. Back in the car to Raleigh Studios. Now it's really hot in the car and I change clothes again. About 40 minutes early, there are signs posted everywhere, "Keep your voices low. Taping auditions in room next door." But, there's a guy sitting here, saying his lines really loud. It's kind of funny. His name's called, he comes out quickly, he looks down, he heads for the elevator. He wasn't in there long. That probably means... what? I go in. Mediocre. There's a picture of an actor I haven't seen in years on the wall. I wonder what he's doing today.

Back in the car, short drive this time. I arrive at Paramount. My name's not on the list. I wait. My appointment's at 2pm and it's only 1:20pm. The security guard says I can't come in until 2pm. I tell him I need to change clothes and work on my script. He doesn't care really, but offers the utility closet for me to change in. I do.

The floor's wet, but I don't realize until my shoes are off. My socks are wet. I hope it's not urine. There's a mop next to me, but I'm not cleaning it up. I walk out of the closet and someone turns around, only to accidentally spill his drink on me. I'm soaked. He says, "Sorry. But it's just water." I can tell he feels bad, I say it's okay. This is the outfit I have to audition in. I'm going to producers for this one.

The security guard takes my ID, checks it out, still can't find my name, makes a few calls, goes through my bag, there's a bra in there, for a different outfit, the one I have to wear next. I don't feel embarrassed, though. Another girl walks up. She's auditioning for the same part. I can tell. She looks familiar. She gives her name. I've done stand-up with her. She doesn't recognize me, and I realize that she's on my email list. I probably shouldn't send emails to people who don't recognize me. I'll take her off the list when I get home. Right?

The guard lets me in. I park my sunny car and take off for the Mae West building. I pass another actress that I know. She just got out of her third callback for the part I auditioned for two auditions ago. I wasn't very good, so I don't feel competitive. She looks nice. I find my room, I sign in. The casting director is late.

Finally! This one goes pretty well. I get some direction. I take it. I feel good. They seem pleased. Great! One more to go! But wait, I need gas. $2.47/gallon. I get some Tofifay candies while I'm at it. I still have my migraine. Am I drinking enough water? I've had two bottles' worth.

Back to Burbank for the next one. I sign in and sit next to a girl who was waiting with me three auditions ago. We smile at each other. I look over my sides. I like this part. I want it. The breakdown says I'm supposed to be plain and plump. I go to the bathroom, change my clothes, take off my earrings, and settle my hair so that I'm plain. Plump? Plump? I look kind of "pillowy," but I don't know about plump. Oh, who cares?

A girl walks in. She's in a commercial that I auditioned for. I hate watching that commercial because it plays all the time and I thought I did a good job at the audition. Oh well. She looks plumper than me. Wait a second; she's here for something else. Who cares? Focus. Okay, I feel good. They take us in late, so I feel confident. The casting director gives me some direction. I do it well. She says, "Great." I know she means it. It felt great.

Time to check in. I call my managers; let them know how each one went. Change clothes again, drive far to a job interview. I'm early. I go window-shopping. Wait, a 99-cent store. I go in. I buy two clipboards, a calculator and some curlers for my hair. It's only $3.99. Wow.

I go to my job interview. I'm fifteen minutes early. She comes out and says she won't be ready for fifteen minutes. When it's time, she welcomes me into her office. It smells bad... like trash. I sit and within five minutes, she tells me I'm not qualified for the job. I know that I am, but why argue at this point? I don't really want to work there. Well, 6pm get back on the freeway, get home by 7pm. My eyes hurt.

It's hard to carry all four pairs of shoes from my car to my apartment. I can feel the remnants of my migraine rattling around in my head. I've got to walk slowly. Apartment: dark. No one's home. I drop my things and try to take a poo. It's somewhat difficult. I guess I'm not hydrated enough. I'll drink some water. I'll watch TV. I wonder if I have any auditions for tomorrow. I feel lucky and tired and hurt and lonely and right. Goodnight.

—Contributed by Crista Flanagan, actor/writer

So... Tell Me About Yourself

You've completed the audition. Or so you thought. You thank the reader, tuck your sides away, and begin to exit the casting room when the casting director stops you, asks you to have a seat, and instructs you to do the most dreaded thing: talk about yourself. This scenario strikes fear in the hearts of the most talented performers. Why?

I once did an interview in which a casting director talked about this. She said the director (yes, the director was in on first audition sessions) asked a young woman to talk a bit about some job she'd had. The director instructed the actor to, "Tell us a funny story. What is it you do?" The young woman, according to the casting director, just froze and stared at the director.

The casting director said to me, "She could've said *anything*! She's an actress! She could just make something up! Anything! Instead, she sat there looking like an idiot until the director turned to me and said, 'Okay. I guess we're finished,' and I had to escort the girl out."

How awful!

I've found the best way to always have something to say is to have experience with improv. I know that improv is really scary to a lot of people, but that is what makes it such a valuable resource for actors. You can think quickly, have responses for just about anything, and usually be pretty funny, once you've learned how to free up the part of you that tries to edit all of that out on a daily basis.

I would suggest, outside of that, that you have a few facts or interesting tidbits in mind, should this happen to you. Here's an example from back in my acting days.

CD: "So, tell me about yourself."

Me: "Hmm... The most unusual thing about me is that I'm a former hand model."

CD: "A *hand model*? Tell me about that."

Me: "Oh, once I had to open a Diet Coke can for an hour, over and over again, for a room full of executives gathered around a conference table. I had to do it slower, faster, with more energy, with more sensuality, and on and on. They had this one can rigged so that I could open it again and again, based on their direction."

CD: "You're kidding."

Me: "No! And once my audition consisted of standing in a line with four other women, each of us holding a fried chicken leg."

CD: "Did you book the job?"

Me: "No. My fingers were too long. I made the chicken leg look tiny. The ad agency *did* end up using me for a pager ad later. I helped their product look tiny!"

We shared a big laugh and the casting director noted on my resumé that I can tell a good story and to this day remembers me as the "hand model girl."

I followed up with a photo postcard that had two photos (one headshot, one hand shot), jogging the memory and thanking the casting director for the audition.

Voila! Small talk.

Asking for Feedback

Step lightly, here. If you have a good relationship with the casting director, her associate, assistant, or intern, feel free to find out if it would be okay to ask for feedback. Don't just ask for feedback outright. Ask whether their office is open to *providing* feedback, then, based on their answer and reaction to the question, decide what the best move would be.

Many casting directors are loathe to give feedback, simply because what actors are really looking for is the answer to the question, "Why didn't you pick me?" The answer to that question has very little to do with your performance as an actor and is really about your type, the director's choices, interpretation of the role (yours and theirs), availability, directability, nepotism, and a zillion other little un-namable things.

If you truly want feedback on your audition and you've been given the go-ahead to ask for it from a friendly casting director or her staff, know how to accept the comments you are given gratefully, graciously, and without any need to defend your choices—even if the feedback seems totally off-target from how you felt the audition went! The last thing anyone in casting wants to do is to defend her choices to an actor. She already has to defend her choices to the director, the producer, and all of her friends and relatives who have asked her to let them read for roles.

Thank the casting director for the feedback and then tuck that information away. If she told you that you didn't look like your headshot, you know how to fix that, right? If she said you buried your head in the sides and auditioned with the top of your head to the camera, get into a good cold reading class to brush up on your audition technique. If she said you read the whole thing as a comedy when it was, in fact, a drama, find out whether you could've done more research before your audition to find that out! If she said, "You're too tall," "You're too young," or "You have the wrong color hair and eyes," let it go. Only focus on what you can learn and apply to the next audition. Feedback is not for the purpose of bargaining your way into that role. That one's gone. Move on.

If the role is not yours, there is nothing you could do that would make it yours.
If the role is yours, there is nothing that can keep you from it.

Publicity

Publicity begins with you. Don't think you need to wait until you're at the level at which one would normally hire a publicist to begin learning the art of publicity and promotion. It's all part of marketing, and you're getting very well-versed on that art, just by reading this book!

Promoting a Show

If you are in a *good* play in Los Angeles, you should plan to invite press and industry to attend. If the play is really only *okay* or your role is tiny, perhaps wait to invite industry to a bigger, better showcase of your talent. Make sure it is a strong production with professional lighting, sound, costumes, and production values of all kinds. Make sure your castmates are strong and you are too, in your performances. Note that casting folks prefer to see as many actors as they can at one time, rather than attending a one-person show, since they can scout more people at a time that way.

Put together a press release announcing the run and well before opening week, fax that to *LA Weekly, LA Times, Curtain Up, Back Stage West, ReviewPlays.com, Daily*

News, Entertainment Today, Theatre LA, NoHo>LA, Tolucan Times (and many other, smaller papers, if there is any valley connection whatsoever). Your press release should include the where, when, who, what, why, all that good stuff. Include a phone number for reservations and a number for comps. Note: most shows get reviewed if they will be running for six weeks, minimum. It just doesn't make sense for a reviewer to see a show in its opening week, have the review come out in the show's second week, and have the show close in week three. So, make sure you have at least a month or more of a run scheduled, to maximize the chances that you get your show reviewed. Once the papers get your press release, reviewers will be assigned to cover the play, and they should get in for free. But, you still want the cost and public reservation line included in your press release, so this information can go in the paper's regular calendar listing. Always have one person listed as the Industry Contact and make sure there's a professional answering service attached to the number you're giving out.

Set up a separate industry comp RSVP phone line so that you will know who is coming to your show and when. Request a business card from industry reps and reviewers when they show up. This allows you to properly identify who gets press kits as well as providing the most current contact information so that you can easily follow up with thank you notes after the show and keep people posted on future events. You are always building a mailing list for future promotional materials!

Call the papers the week of the opening (which should be at least two weeks after they've received your press release). Ask if they'd like a press kit or stills from the show to run with the review you're hoping they'll do. Be ready to provide those, if that offer is accepted. Make sure you're on their "to review" list and, if you can, find out who's doing the review, so you'll have someone ready to meet and greet that person the night of the show.

Of course, the best way to get a review is to have good buzz about your show "out there." So, don't just focus on getting the papers out. Do a little more legwork, if you can. Create flyers. Whatever your design is, make it clean and easy to read. Include the pertinent information here as well, and get this flyer *everywhere*. Have cast, crew, classmates, and friends help paper the town, stack flyers (or smaller postcard versions) in every performance space, rehearsal space, casting studio, and industry hangout you know of.

If you can spare the funds, put your flyer in Breakdown Services' announcement section. They will include it with the Breakdowns that go out to hundreds of subscribing agents and managers. Again, provide lots of contact information and have a clean, professional look.

About two weeks before the opening, send out postcards inviting everyone already on your ever-growing mailing list to come see the show. If there is no official show postcard produced by the theatre, use one of your own photo postcards and write on it all of the pertinent information (show name, dates, times, theatre location, phone number for industry comps). You should use the most current *CD Directory* from Breakdown Services and the latest copy of *The Agencies* from Acting World Books to ensure you have current addresses. Make sure that you have a phone number on the postcards for industry comps.

In order to promote the show to people in the industry to whom you are a stranger, begin by gathering press materials from the show (flyers, postcards, press releases put together by the producers, cast bios) as well as any good press the show has already received (if it is open and has been reviewed by anyone). Put together a little packet with your headshot, resumé, and a professional cover letter, then send that to the people you most want there. Make sure again to provide a phone number to call for industry comps.

Yes, most industry folks will know that there are comps, but you need to make it easy for them to see how to get them.

Keep in mind that industry folks get invited to every show going on in town every day. Make your invitation stand out by having the most professional presentation you can afford. Make sure the press kits—available upon request and at the ticket window—match the theme and design of the postcards you sent out. Press kits include headshots and resumés, bios, programs, flyers, and any press you've already received. Make them look good! These kits are what the casting people will take away with them, along with notes they make during your performance.

As with anything like this, it's hard to know exactly what impact a mailing has on actual attendance. I think you have to view the mailing as more of an investment in your reputation as a working actor. Sending show invitations helps to remind the casting directors that you are *out there working* and to keep them informed of it. In the long term, they are an investment in the way you are perceived by these folks.

Note that casting directors don't always want to be recognized in public. They may attend your shows without identifying themselves as industry, pay full price, sit quietly, scribble notes about the actors in the playbill, and head home without you ever even knowing it. Happens all the time!

Increasing the Odds

Start by putting on a show in a convenient location. Even though you may really believe in your little black-box theatre space with the alley entrance, it's pretty unlikely that a casting director is going to brave the unknown to see your show, especially when invited to mainstream, popular venues for that same night.

Don't make it a hassle for industry to get comps and press kits. It has to be incredibly easy for the casting director to call in a reservation, have free passes waiting at the door, and receive a press kit filled with the headshots and resumés of the actors upon arrival. They're busy people, and often will leave during intermission. This doesn't mean they're not enjoying the show. Often it means they're headed back to the office to add your name to a list they're handing off to a director or producer the following morning.

Get those reviews out! If the show has been reviewed by one of the local papers, a copy of that review should be sent to casting directors. If they receive indications that the night would not be a waste of time, they're more likely to see the show.

Some theatres will do special industry nights, in which many casting directors, agents, managers, producers, and directors are invited to a catered affair, with valet parking and a no-host bar, all of which factors will drive traffic to the show. Are you bribing people to come to the show? No. You are presenting a special night just for them, knowing they won't have time to get dinner between leaving the office and coming to your show, knowing they'll be in a rush to find parking, and knowing—upon seeing their colleagues— they will most likely want to have a cocktail and schmooze a bit.

The Bottom Line

Yes, this is getting expensive, but this multi-tiered approach to marketing is the best way to get (and keep) the attention of casting directors and agents you want to attend your shows. I know you don't want to know this, but return on investment for all this publicity is actually pretty low, unless you're involved in something that casting directors were planning to attend already. That's why you shouldn't look at the cost-benefit ratio on publicity. It has a cumulative impact. And remember, you are in this for the long haul!

I know this publicity stuff is also very work-intensive. If you don't have the time or money to do it all the way, don't feel bad! These are just suggestions for the *best* way to promote your show, if money and time were no object. Having the energy to do all the legwork should never be an issue because you should always find the energy to further your career and live your dreams!

The last show I directed and produced had an advertising budget of whatever I saved by brown-bagging my lunch for the month, so you definitely can do publicity with a limited budget. We got reviewed everywhere and had industry turn out each night of the show's run. One of the actors in my show got called in by the William Morris Agency after opening night (a rep was there) and two more of the cast members got called in by casting directors for pilots the following month, based on the flyers I had mailed out. Publicity does work!

The Personal Touch

While it may seem to be a silly little issue, many casting directors I've interviewed really hate pre-printed address labels. They feel that the postcards are coming from someone they've never met and someone who has no interest in making a personal invitation to the people in the office. I'm not sure that it's all that big a deal. While a handwritten address on a printed postcard is far more personal, even handwriting a note on a postcard on which you've used a pre-printed address label can make a difference. The casting director will glance at it and think, "Hmm... have we met?" Just a thought.

When To Hire a Publicist

There will be a time when you need to hire a publicist to do your promotion for you. To get perspective on that timing—and other issues involved with hiring someone *else* to do your publicity—I revisited a panel discussion I attended on that very subject.

Led by moderator Michael Levine—owner of Levine Communications Office and author of *Guerrilla PR*—a panel of four industry professionals shared their wit and wisdom on the art of publicity, its importance to a performer's career, and a few of the nitty-gritty details involved in PR in a wonderful discussion sponsored by the Talent Managers Association.

Maryann Ridini, president of Ridini Entertainment Corporation, said an actor should hire a publicist, "Several months before the film, the TV show, the record comes out. The campaign has to be put together and planned. There's the writing of the press kit, collection of materials, schedule of releases. If they're in a film, you want to have a six-month lead-time to put the media list together and tailor it to the target audience. So often, I have people come to me just one month prior to their project, which really limits us."

Levine asked the panel of experts, "Should the public relations firm put out a proposal for no fee?"

Kenneth R. Reynolds, president and CEO of Public Relations+, responded, "It depends on the circumstances. Once, I did a free proposal for a church and it was just an outline. They came back to me and asked me to firm it up, put in a few more details. I did. They came back again, asking for further elaboration and I'm thinking, 'Y'know, church is very big business.' But, I did it anyway, and they said, based on that third proposal, 'Our secretary could do this.' Well, of course. At that point, she could."

Deborah Berger, partner and publicist at DBPR,

added, "Corporate accounts seem to want proposals more than specific celebrities. With entertainers, we're generally paid up front, rather than on commission. We have a lot to prove, by having already earned our money. We prove our relationships. That's our forte."

Ridini commented, "It depends on what you put in the proposal. Many people don't know how it works, so you have to educate them on how you do what you do. Have a good relationship with your publicist. Know how they're going to work."

"What are the fee structures?" Levine inquired.

"From $1,000 to $5,000 per month," Reynolds offered.

Berger concurred. "Roughly the same range. The higher end is more corporate or more handholding, more travel. The lower end is more maintenance. Maybe they're not in need of major publicity but they want to attend a premiere, they want to attend a party, they want to attend a fashion event. Keep in mind, this fee is plus expenses. Always."

"Oh, yes, that's important to note," Reynolds agreed. "So often, the client thinks expenses are included. It's like the contract is signed, but not read, because it's in there. There's the photographer payment, there's the FedEx bill, there's postage, there's supplies, and they think I should assume those costs. No, I am paid for what I *know*. Be very clear. Put it in the contract. If you are paying me a fee, and then I pay the photographer out of my fee, and then I pay for reproductions, and I pay the writers to write your bio, and I pay for copies of the bio, where do I get paid for what I know?"

"The range depends on what we do for the client," Ridini clarified. "If they want national press, international press, doing a book in certain cities, it varies. Blanket statements are difficult to make, but I'd say $2,500 to

$10,000 for corporations."

Our fourth panelist, Nelson Aspen—a correspondent for TV Guide Television and the number one morning show in the UK—teaches Media Training at The Learning Annex, is my co-host for Hollywood Happy Hour, and offers private coaching in Multi-Media Essentials. "As a promoter, rather than a publicist," he began, "there is money in my pocket to promote other people. Why I do media training is because there is this question of *when* publicity begins. Media training is money well spent. You spend money on your acting classes, your headshots, and you should also spend on knowing when and how to promote yourself. I do private coaching for $100 per hour. It is purely instructional."

Mistakes People Make in Dealing with Publicists

"There's a lack of feeding information," Reynolds explained. "They take it for granted that there is something going on in the entertainer's life that could be used for publicity. It's not an act of withholding, it's just that they are not judging that it's useful information to us."

"I find that managers don't believe in publicity," Berger added. "It's another person in the mix, it's another cost. That comes from a power and control factor. Actors have an agent, they have a manager, they have a business manager, they have an attorney, and you're another person in the mix, advising them and working their public image."

"Actors need to know that the time to hire a publicist is when you have a story to tell," Reynolds summarized.

Aspen elaborated, "Everybody has a story to tell. But make sure it's venue-appropriate. I'm always looking for evergreen stories; stories that our show can re-run for the next three years. We'll do anything on *Frasier* but *Gideon's Crossing* was tougher to book. The spin is the important thing."

"If the series got on the air, even if it's quickly canceled, at least it got on the air. A lead should have a publicist to take advantage of the time it's out there," Ridini noted.

"The press kit alone could get them their next job," Aspen agreed.

Berger explained the complexity of layered promotional efforts. "Many times, an actor's desire to get publicity is overshadowed by network involvement. They want to wait to see how it's going to do before investing in publicity."

Manager Kathy Boole of Studio Talent Group asked, "What is the negotiation process? Are we guaranteed that we'll get our money's worth?"

Reynolds replied, "I cannot promise you'll be in a certain publications. But I can promise I'll do my best to make it happen. I'll use every bit of knowledge and creativity at my disposal to make it happen."

Levine continued the theme of Boole's question, adding, "And if a publicist promises that you'll be in a certain publication...?"

Reynolds quickly responded, "Run."

"It's not guaranteed," Berger added.

"You should look for a publicist with relationships," Aspen suggested. "I am such a fan of nepotism. It works!"

Manager Art Mines asked, "Do you make concessions, in your fees, for charitable causes?"

"In any business, we do charitable giving. We do campaigns pro bono for certain causes. We give a lot," Reynolds insisted.

"I was watching *Oprah* in my office the other day," Aspen began, "and she gave money to Camp Heartland, this camp for kids with AIDS. I see a story there that's waiting to happen, so I call the guy, and pitch a story, even before calling my editor to make sure it'll happen. So, if you have a story, make it happen. And, yes, this one is for free."

Manager Horacio Blackwood, owner of Blackwood Entertainment asked, "What are your tips on finding a good publicist?"

Berger responded, "Referrals, definitely, from other managers."

Aspen added, "Referrals from talent."

Reynolds joined in, "Referrals from journalists."

Ridini completed the list: "Referrals from studios."

How Actors Can Make a Publicist's Job Easier

"Return calls in a timely manner," Berger requested. "Our job is time-sensitive. We're on a deadline and we can't say, 'I'm sorry, she's with her shrink right now, so I can't get you that headshot.' Also, don't forget your interviews. If I've scheduled an interview for you, show up for it!"

"Take your publicist's advice on how to deal with the media," Ridini suggested. "You hired us for our expertise."

"Make sure you sit down with your publicist and get an understanding of what the relationship is, what the publicist's job is. Know that I am not a marketing director," Reynolds added.

Aspen explained that, "Actors, unless they're very experienced, treat publicity like a luxury. It is not a luxury. It has the same import as all the other ingredients to your career. Publicity is not a perk."

Manager Helen Cohen asked, "What about having the actor, the manager, the publicist, the agent, all in the same room, so that you're assured you're all headed for the same result?"

Ridini began, "I generally operate where I meet with those team members, but we all have our area of expertise. Yes, there are shared goals, but we have to work from our own strengths, each of us on the team. You don't want duplication of efforts. There may be an undercurrent in Hollywood of us not getting along, but we can work together."

Berger added, "You CC everybody and their mother. You leave a paper trail. Show everyone what you're trying to do. It can't be a bad thing for me to CC the president of the network. He may throw away the memo, but it can't hurt for him to see that my client is getting out there, doing press. CC webmasters of fansites too."

Manager Lola Blank, owner of LHB Management asked, "Would you ever tell an actor that a publicist is no longer necessary?"

"It's a touchy area because you're basically saying, 'I don't want your money.' But, if there's nothing going on in the client's life, it comes to a point where you've exhausted everything you can," Reynolds explained.

Manager David Moore of Alliance Models said, "I've never hired a publicist. Where does the money we use to pay you come from?"

Reynolds said, "Ultimately, it comes from the talent."

"The money comes from the project," Ridini clarified. "Whatever you—the actor—are working on, it pays you, and you pay us from that. You have to be realistic. If you're not working, and you're not bringing in money, you don't need a publicist."

"That's when I do maintenance," Berger added. "I'll half my retainer fee."

"You can hire us for consulting work," Ridini said. "Actors could come in and pay $85 to $100 per hour to get my expertise."

Manager Denise Ellis of G Talent asked, "Who writes the press release?"

Berger said, "We all do."

Ridini agreed, "Any good publicist should be a good writer."

"It's unbelievable to me," Aspen began, "the number of press releases I see with typos and misspellings. It's unreal to me!"

Manager and comedy coach Steve Kaplan said, "I work with people where the story is good but the money is not there yet. What can we do?"

"They should choose consultation over a retainer," Ridini advised.

Moderator Levine began, "I wrote a book called *Guerrilla PR*, which is the most widely-used introduction for PR. It's based on The Tiffany Theory, which is essentially that a little blue box means more to you than a plain box. In our society, we gift-wrap everything, even our toilet paper."

Berger agreed. "Look at a publicist and the way they work at media and red carpets events. If they're letting their stars show up in black or grey and with no jewelry, they're saying they don't want to be photographed. I'm thrilled when someone shows up with a blue box of an outfit."

Manager Linda Reitman asked, "When an actor is doing indie films and you don't really have a release date, can you do anything for them?"

"We really need a release date so that we can move from that date to make sure to get the most coverage," Ridini insisted.

Manager Doyle Taylor of Down Right Talented asked, "Do you feel you can resurrect a client's career or image?"

"If they have a project pending, yes," Ridini said. "You need to have a vehicle or there is no news hook. There's so many stories out there. Journalists want to be sure there's a hook. So, it must be more than a human-interest story."

Manager David Westberg asked, "Has the Internet complicated your job?"

Aspen responded, "It's awesome. The more the better! But you have to police it. Sometimes performers will go into chat rooms to generate some buzz."

"With the Internet, the laws don't exist yet," Berger affirmed. "There are bookers who will go online and pull bios that aren't official. There's a lack of control there."

Cohen asked, "Do you participate in damage-control campaigns? Do you develop an A to Z strategy?"

"Absolutely!" Berger exclaimed. "I'll work from A to T then see what happens from T to Z. It's part of the job, damage control, but you want to reserve some of the resources for future publicity."

Manager Betty McCormick Aggas of Midwest Talent posed the question, "What's an average day for you?"

Berger began, "I check my cell phone, check my voicemail, check my email, check my faxes. I try to put out any fires and then I go to my list and work everything that's pending. I have all of these Internet relationships and it's made my life so much easier. I highly recommend subscribing to the Hollywood News Calendar, it's worth the $100 per month, to make you aware of all the book signings, all the premieres, and you can receive it by email or fax, and you can get your clients out to these events, and they love it."

Aspen summarized his average day simply, stating, "It's the best!"

Gratitude

Many people have asked me—a good Southern Belle who believes thank you notes are *always* appropriate—what the best methods of expressing appreciation are here in Hollywood. Should you send a thank you note for every audition? Probably not. Should you send a thank you note when you've been called in against type or someone has taken a risk on you? Absolutely. Should you send a thank you note when you book a role? Without a doubt! Flowers are nice too—if you've booked a national commercial or a series regular role.

As for me, the only thing I ever request of people who find my advice helpful is this: just give me a shout-out when you accept your Oscar, your Emmy, your Tony, your People's Choice Award. I'll be watching you give your acceptance speech, and to hear a little "thank you" would just send me on a thrill ride like you wouldn't believe!

Back to the more traditional display of gratitude: the thank you note. Short and sweet is plenty. Send a photo postcard (or even a traditional thank you card with your photo business card inside) saying, "Just wanted to thank you for bringing me in for the role of _____. I really enjoyed meeting you and hope to work with you soon!"

If you shared a "moment" over anything in particular, you can note that here too ("I hope your son is feeling better. I know you were concerned about him during our meeting," "Good luck with the renovations on your office," "Hope you get a nice vacation soon," for example). But don't push it. If you had a plain, flat-out good audition, say thank you for that. Make sure your goal is to say "thank you," not to kiss butt.

Unique gifts are appreciated when appropriate. A friend of mine orders custom-made headshot labels for gourmet products, so that the gift baskets, wine, and the like, are also a means of getting his face out there, just one more time. I think casting directors like things they can use (and if that's gourmet coffee or creamer or some packaged goods, that's a good idea). I know that one casting director was very amused by—but not at all interested in hiring—the guy who gave him a coffee mug with his headshot on it. So, expendables with your promotional photo may be a better balance.

A dear friend of mine bakes an amazing Coca-Cola Cake and she gave mini-cakes to a few casting directors at the winter holiday season a couple of years ago. One casting director said to me, later, "As much as I like [her] and am sure this is a fine cake, I cannot accept food from actors."

She indicated that the idea of "something slipped in" was just too strong to ignore. I was surprised, but then realized it's not that different from parents discouraging kids from eating unwrapped Halloween candy given out by strangers. So save the baked goods for casting directors with whom you have a more solid relationship.

So, don't spend too much money, and make your offering memorable (but in a good way). Also, remember that a thank you note goes the distance, in terms of earning respect. The gifts aren't really necessary, but true gratitude most definitely is.

Attitude counts. I was watching that damn show The It Factor *and [one actor] didn't get either part. Watching her demeanor, it seemed obvious to me why she was not cast. Her attitude, in a nutshell, sucks. I'd rather work my way up and eventually be able to [say no to certain roles]. Until then, listen, I have no problem being the new face of genital herpes if it means I get a paycheck and exposure.*

—Danielle Twin-Smucker, actor

Part Six: Living

Survival Jobs

Before you read another word here, if you're serious about getting a survival job, pick up Deborah Jacobson's *Survival Jobs: 154 Ways To Make Money While Pursuing Your Dreams.* That book is just plain amazing for the working actor in Los Angeles who still needs to supplement his income.

Temping

Almost all companies in this town are actor-friendly, as long as you are professional, punctual, and willing to give plenty of notice when you know you'll be unavailable for work due to auditions or performances. Most companies are thrilled to have an enthusiastic, skilled employee and are willing to give a little time off and flexibility in order to keep that person on staff as long as possible.

That said, I've heard of plenty of temp agencies that say, "Do not tell the company you're an actor," but I think that the temp agencies themselves don't mind a bit. Besides, everyone knows everyone is shopping some other lifestyle around. It's all a matter of how on-task you are while in "their" world.

I was the office manager for a small temp agency in 1999. Its staff was almost entirely made up of actors and the agency sent folks out exclusively within the industry. What I learned while there was that the temp agencies are getting a *ton* more for you per hour than you take home. You would be much better off getting your own gigs. Of course, that requires that you be entrepreneurial. More and more entertainment companies are using in-house temps, so check out the various studios' and production companies' job lines (all listed at EntertainmentCareers.net) for information on how to get in their temp pools.

If you're working at a studio or other entertainment industry temp job, if you are asked whether you have any interest in acting, you could certainly share your aspirations. Just don't go spilling headshots all over the floor!

Teaching

Another survival job that is popular with actors is substitute teaching. I worked as a sub for two school years. It's a good gig. I have a friend who subs in Burbank and he could work pretty much every day if he wanted to. I think that's especially the case here, where year-round school options exist. Schools are always glad to get a good, reliable sub (and your name will get passed around pretty quickly).

If academic work is your thing, but you don't like the idea of a full day with many students, you may want to get registered with a tutorial service. This is another survival job I've had. There are several companies that do SAT-prep and straight-out academic tutoring all over town providing excellent pay and great flexibility. Most tutorial services want tutors to come in and take their SAT-prep course to learn their "method" and that way, you're set to tutor either academic subjects or teach the SAT course one-on-one. That gives you more opportunity to work.

Again, you'll make more money on your own than you do going through an agency, but that—again—requires an entrepreneurial spirit and access to the families most likely to hire independent tutors.

Freelancing

Freelancing requires a good bit of organizational skill and a great memory for names and faces. You don't ever want to "drop" a contact. You have no idea how valuable it can be, down the line. Of course, working a room and remembering names and faces is a key part of marketing yourself as an actor too, so this skill will serve you well in several arenas.

My "path" looks a lot more like a random zigzag through the industry, but I can tell you that it has really worked for me. I know a lot about computers, so—while pursuing acting—I started doing freelance work, teaching senior citizens how to send email to their grandkids, installing software for the technophobic, building the occasional webpage. Los Angeles is pretty behind the curve, technologically, so—if you are a geek like I am—clients will pass your name around until you're having to turn away all the people who need tutorials. That's a great feeling! But, it takes a while. I had to get very poor between my temping gig and the time when freelancing began to really pay off. But I wouldn't trade it!

One of my freelance clients owns a college textbook publishing company. A very mom-and-pop place, extremely casual, and the most flexible company I have ever encountered. They hire everyone at an extremely low rate to start, but raises come very fast, once they find out they can count on you. Jobs range from packing books into boxes to copy-editing from home. I went from doing research on professors in-house to designing and managing the company's online presence and shopping cart.

My job with *Back Stage West* began when the casting department started calling me in to do as-needed data entry work when staff members went on vacation. Then they asked me to transcribe some interview tapes from home, when staff writers needed help. Within a few months, it became known around the office that I had a "secret" Master's degree in Journalism and I was asked to pen my weekly column, *Casting Qs* which became my recent book—and eventually, all that work interviewing casting directors turned into a career as a casting director!

The beauty of freelancing is, no matter what, you pick and choose your work. I was happy to just be in a new environment each day—and by being reliable and flexible, I've made a career out of the various favorite jobs I've had. I worked for the Sundance Institute freelance for a year and then co-founded a short film festival! I met Nelson Aspen and Kris Burtt in the course of one of my freelance gigs and we founded Hollywood Happy Hour!

While I was piecing various jobs together into a career of my own, I also tutored kids, house-sat, baby-sat, pet-sat, designed webpages, created educational software, worked as a paid studio audience member for TV shows, and I even taught traffic school for the Improv Comedy Club! Have fun with your survival jobs. I sure did!

What's Best for You?

Freelance working requires discipline and focus. It's not for everyone. If you decide to be a temp, register with multiple companies. Be available. On the days you don't temp, ask the agency if you can come in and improve your skills on their computers. They will notice the effort and reward you with the best jobs. Also, you'll get better-paying jobs when your skills improve.

The Job Factory is a service you pay for, but it pays for itself with the first job you get, which is guaranteed. If you take in the *Working Actor's Guide* and a headshot, you get 20% off (making registration $45, I think). I don't know that the money for each job is much better than with temping, but there are certainly more listings at The Job Factory than with most temp agencies on any given day, mainly because the companies don't have to pay for the service, like they do when they hire you through traditional temp agencies. Most companies pay cash on the day you work. That's a biggie! Most of it is "one day" work, meaning you won't have to deal with taxes or anything. They have long-term stuff, too, but it's all very non-traditional. The guys who started the company in 1970 were UCLA students frustrated with the temp scene in Los Angeles. The company is very understanding of the flexibility required in an actor's life. Again, though, it *working* relies on your ability to be proactive.

There's a legend going around about Vin Diesel and his ability to earn and save $47,000 as a telemarketer before he made it big. First, let me say that telemarketing is *hard* work. The most important thing to focus on in that story about *all that money* is this: not only did Diesel earn $47,000 in his first year in Los Angeles by telemarketing, he saved every penny he could. He said that he watched other aspiring actors buying hot cars, renting big apartments, throwing parties, dressing nice, and going out all the time. He knew that doing those things would be fun, but would also put him at a greater distance from attaining his dream.

So, he drove his old car, wore the same clothes every other day, and lived in a tiny single while he saved his money to invest it in his self-produced film. That film was what got Steven Spielberg on the phone to him. It's not just the *earning* that makes a difference, it's the *investment* in yourself as an actor.

Market Research

Market research and focus groups are not only easy money, but they're fun! When I was working as an actor, I was registered with several big recruiting groups in Los Angeles and I developed a "must" list, for being called back to do market research and focus groups again and again.

First: whenever you are called for the prescreening, you must state that it has been at least six months since your last participation in a market research study or focus group of any kind.

Next: you are not in the entertainment, advertising, or marketing industries, nor do you know anyone employed by the research firm, the company it is studying, or the ad agency sponsoring the study.

The range of pay is from $5 per 10-minute online survey to $200 for a six-hour stint on a mock jury, where selection is based on demographics (political leanings, education level, race, age, marital status). You must name, as your employer, a company that would pay you while serving on a jury (even if they wouldn't) and the bigger the company, the better. They will not verify employment, but you do need to at least temp or freelance with the company you list.

Online surveys come from websites like iopinion.com and acop.com, among many others. Checks for $5 to $25 are paid by mail, four to six weeks after completing online surveys. Plaza Research (iopinion.com) also provides take-home studies for products. Pay for take-home studies is generally $35 to $50, paid upon the return of survey materials and empty containers. Adept Market Research also does take-home studies for $50 to $75. You must be invited to participate in their research groups, however.

Schlesinger Associates, Qualitative Insights, and Southern California Interviewing Service are other popular

Los Angeles market research and focus group companies. You may be asked to be a member of a test audience for a new TV show, you may be shown advertising for a product that doesn't yet exist, or you may sit with other people and discuss how a certain fragrance makes you feel. There are many other companies popping up all the time, as well as many online research companies that pledge payment for survey completion. Shop around and earn a few extra bucks here and there, just for sharing your opinion!

Also Cool

Parts modeling is a neat little industry-like job. I am a former hand model. I registered my hands with various "parts" agencies that work along with "body doubles" and "fit models," rather than with traditional talent agencies. I got a lot of hand modeling work—much that you would recall having seen—while my hands were younger. This is great fun and very unusual, for a survival job—but if you have good parts: go for it!

Another fun job is filling empty seats at award shows. Seatfiller.com is a site where you can sign up ahead of time (with headshot, resumé, and cover letter stating your interest in becoming a seat filler). You'll be contacted whenever shows open up with the need for your services. You'll get short notice and you'll be asked to wear appropriate upscale clothing. You'll have to be patient and smiling regularly, while filling those seats. And no, you don't get to schmooze with the celebs.

Game shows are great fun—and there is a lot of money to win! While you're used to seeing network game shows come and go—among the granddaddies of game shows—you may be less aware of the fact that the Game Show Network produces original game show programming regularly. Watch the shows, check the final credits for information on where the shows tape and how to become a contestant, get registered, and—even if you're a union actor— you could get on several different shows and win cash and fabulous prizes!

As for extra work, here's the deal: just as I started this chapter with a book recommendation, I'll end with one too. If you have any interest in extra work whatsoever—and yes, extra work is more akin to a survival job than an acting gig—you must pick up a copy of the Hollywood OS book *Extra Work for Brain Surgeons.* A new edition comes out each year spelling out all the rules, clarifying all the expectations you should have, and debunking all the myths about extra work you may have learned so far.

Soaps

Soap casting directors have far less time for general auditions or interviews than casting directors of other projects, so I'm giving them their own chapter. Why do they have less time to see actors for generals? Well, it's mainly because they are busy casting a show that shoots 48 to 49 weeks per year! Many agents and managers assume their clients aren't interested in soaps (especially if the actor has a strong theatre resumé), so—if you are represented and you want to do soap work—you'll need to make your interest known.

If you haven't already been on the set of a soap opera, I strongly recommend that you do some extra work on a soap. The casting directors for extras are usually not the same as the casting directors for contract roles. Check with AFTRA for its listings of each soap and then submit your headshot and resumé accordingly. It's important that you get some on-set experience so you'll learn what it is that casting directors are looking for. And, as extra work goes, soap sets are some of the best working conditions in the industry!

While there are stories of soap extras who have made it in good with the AD and gotten bumped up to U5 roles, don't count on that happening. Just go to that set ready to learn, be professional, and have fun. Most soaps have hotlines set up for extras (these are all listed in *Extra Work for Brain Surgeons*), so make sure you call in regularly to state your availability, once you're on their radar. Some soap extra casting departments want weekly calls from actors (*Days of Our Lives*, I know for sure expects weekly calls) and others—such as *Passions*—accept only a biweekly check-in from actors. When you call in, identify yourself, provide your phone number, and list the days of the coming week(s) when you are available for work. Be professional and courteous and make sure you don't rush through your phone number. Make it easy for them to call you in.

Now, you may have to call the hotline every week (or every two weeks, depending on the soap) for about three months before you get your first call in. Once they have a "big crowd" need, you'll get called in. Once they know they can count on you, on-set, they'll call again pretty soon for a smaller casting need. That's always good (more money).

It's hard to get used to calling in, but pick a regular time (like every Tuesday night, for example) and call in, give your availability for the next week, and go on about your life. That's another ritual to set up. And another thing to let go of, once it's done each week.

When you get called in, take something to read while you're waiting and pack a bottle of water and some low-maintenance snack foods. You could have a long day ahead of you, and you don't want to be in the way, nor do you want to leave a mess behind. Make friends and network, but don't get into the big gossip machine that seems to exist on many sets. It will not serve you well for more than a moment. Finally, remember: the major benefit to doing soap extra work is that it's fun, it's a relatively short day, and the pay is very good.

Hosting

I couldn't think of anyone better-suited to tackle the issue of on-camera hosting than Kris Burtt, who has sold many a bauble on ShopNBC in addition to working dozens of other host gigs while pursuing her acting career. She contributed the following step-by-step guide to a successful hosting life.

Five Steps To Becoming Guy Smiley

Okay, so you have moved to Los Angeles to pursue a career in entertainment. You do not act, you do not write, you do not want to direct, you do not want to do hair and makeup, nor do you want to produce. What are you going to do? Have you considered becoming an on-camera host? It is one of the best-kept secrets in the entertainment industry. With the explosion of reality-based television shows, the need for on-camera hosts to drive the shows has also boomed. There are so many different genres that need hosts: game shows, entertainment shows, reality shows, industrial films, home shopping shows, variety shows, and children's programming... the list goes on and on. Here are my five steps for mapping out your path in the crazy world of hosting.

1. Training

How do you train to become a host? Hosting is truly about showing different colors of your own personality— the fun side, the serious side, or the most informative version of you. Like with acting, it is so important to understand who you are, to be a good host. Are you the girl-next-door or the glamorous type? How about the sporty jock or the frat boy? It is crucial to understand how you come across to casting directors and agents so that you can market yourself in the most successful way possible.

A way to discover those aspects of your personality is to take a host class. I bet you didn't even know host classes existed, did you? Marki Costello of CMEG (a host management company) runs a Host Boot Camp Weekend that takes you through the paces of hosting different genres. From game show to co-hosting, you will understand what it takes to nail that audition. Carol Elizabeth Barlow, a casting director in Los Angeles, also offers host seminars to help get you started. I studied with Joan See in New York. Her spokesperson class breaks down the basic aspects of industrial copy and helps you achieve a presence when delivering vast quantities of information. If you aren't sure whether this is useful... well, I parlayed my host training into a job as spokesperson for Toyota on the auto show circuit, which then led to a job as co-host on Seattle's PAX network for the Vintage Vehicle Show.

For those of you with broadcast journalism degrees, you are definitely on the right track. So many of today's cable networks look for a host who is able to write, shoot, and edit his or her own material. People with news backgrounds are often trained to use the IFB (the earpiece that allows the producer or director to talk to the talent while on the air) and have great experience with live broadcasts. *My college degree is in dance, so I have taken the time to utilize the UCLA Extension program to brush up on my writing and broadcast journalism skills. In the journalism category, interviewing is an area that will always be a part of your host career. Learning to prepare for an interview and strengthening your listening skills will only put you at the top of the pack.*

When I lived in New York, I also studied TelePrompTer and ear-prompter skills. A TelePrompTer allows the script to be posted in front of the lens of the television camera. The trick is to make your read as natural-looking as possible. An ear-prompter allows you to record the script in your own voice on a micro-cassette recorder. This recording is then piped into your ear, where you hear the script about two seconds before you recite it. Using the ear-prompter takes more concentration skills and, I must admit, it was a challenge for me to learn. Having these skills has made me more marketable for the industrial film and live industrial segments of the business. TelePrompTer skills are crucial to hosting on camera, but ear-prompter proficiency has only broadened my job prospects.

The other class I would recommend is improvisation. So many of the host auditions include ad-libbing the script. You have to be able to deliver the information in a clear, concise way, but in your own words. If you are working with a co-host, another important skill is to be able to banter. Just watch Regis and Kelly *or* The View *for a great example of how your improvisation skills come into play. Not only do you have to listen to your co-host, but since these shows are broadcast live, the element of surprise is always there.*

I have thrown out numerous ways to train and prepare for your host career. Do not be overwhelmed by the possibilities. Take it one step at a time and figure out what would be the best path for you. I started with the spokesperson class, and then followed it up with ear-prompter and TelePrompTer training. I signed up for the on-camera host class and realized that my improv skills needed some work. When I felt ready to hit the audition circuit, I beefed up my resumé with the broadcast journalism classes. It became a natural progression for me, but it did not happen overnight. It was a journey that began in 1998 and continues to this day!

2. Headshots, Resumés, Reels

Your hosting headshot should resemble you. Right now, I hear you saying, "Duh!" But—as Bonnie has emphasized—so many casting directors will tell you that the person who often walks through their door does not resemble his or her picture. In essence, you want your photo to capture your energy. This will be a part of your entire PR package. You want the personality of your photo to carry over to your reel, which carries over to your bio. It is really that important to understand who you are as a host.

Your resumé should resemble an acting resumé in regards to organization and setup. There are certain items that I highlight on my resumé that I think are important for a casting director or producer to know. For instance, my TelePrompTer, IFB, and ear-prompter proficiency tells the casting director that I can give the crew options on how to deliver the information through me to the viewing audience. I also have professional dance training as well as experience teaching dance classes to children. This led to a fabulous job hosting a children's dance video! As mentioned before, my knowledge of cars resulted in a hosting gig, and I'm still trying to parlay my figure skating obsession into a host job. You never know where your skills will take you, so even if you can recite every color of a

Crayola Crayon 68-pack, there is probably a show out there for you to host.

When it comes to your reel for hosting, this is a vital part of your marketing package. You will use your reel all the time. Unlike an actor's demo reel, your host reel will almost always be submitted along with your headshot. It is often the first thing casting directors ask for, and they may prescreen who they'll call in based on tapes. Again, you want your reel to reflect your personality. I most often get hired as your high energy, wacky-yet-informative host who services the project with a sense of fun.

If you are just starting out, you probably do not have tape. This is where you can show your creativity and demonstrate who you are. Write some copy, choose your locations, and go shoot with a crew. If you want to do entertainment shows, go stand outside a movie premiere and cover it. You will not get access to the stars, but you will be able to use the action in the background to your advantage. If you are an extreme sports fanatic, interview snowboarders at an event, go to a skateboard park, or even jump into the action yourself. The opportunities are endless, but invest your time and money wisely in this reel. This is not the time to cut corners or do it as inexpensively as possible. Save up your money and create a quality reel that will make a casting director call you in for a project.

That also means finding a good editor to help you capture your hosting personality. You do not want long, drawn-out cuts on this tape. In fact, more MTV-style editing is preferable in the hosting world. Remember, this is your calling card. Deliver one that you are proud to show to everyone. It should be updated regularly once you begin working. I update mine as often as three times a year to keep it fresh for casting directors as well as for myself. So, if your training is progressing in the right direction, get out there and shoot!

3. Marketing

Okay, you now have your tools ready to go. Starting with all the preparation Bonnie has given you, you now have to specifically market yourself as a host. There are a million ways to do that, so I will throw just a couple of ideas out to you. Hopefully, this will inspire you to create even more interesting ways to get your name and face out there.

First and foremost, postcards are your basic tools. They are vital to actors and they can be vital to hosts. I send my postcards out every four to six weeks even though I am currently employed as a host of a regular show. There are always updates to mention: the airing of my shows, my new host reel, or even the launch of my website. It is the easiest way to communicate your news by reaching hundreds with one little stamp.

The second way to grab attention is to have a PR kit. I assemble a biography, resumé, headshot, my reel, and any articles written about me into a folder. You can be creative here. You really should have the same theme running throughout each piece. I market myself as fun and high-energy. That idea is translated through a headshot with personality, a quick-paced host reel, a humorous bio (or, at least, my attempt at humor), and a presentation package with color—no use of black, dark blue, or brown. If you can carry that idea throughout your marketing instruments, the casting director or producer will "get" you. It eliminates any guesswork about who you are or what your place is in the host world. Can I tell you how many times I have been hired because I offer a complete PR package? It really astounds me how many comments I get. The extra few dollars I invest in my career has allowed me to stand out in a crowded field.

As a host, having a business card is a must! I have exchanged business cards in airports, children's birthday parties, and at the Mall of America. Being an on-camera host is a very unique position in the entertainment industry. People are intrigued when I tell them what I do. There are so many ways to be employed as a host: live events, industrial films, and television, just to name a few. Grab the opportunity to sell yourself. You never know who needs an emcee at a charity event or a spokesperson at a tradeshow. This may not be the television show that you ultimately want, but doing it gives you the opportunity to practice your skills and open more doors to your host career. So, grab those business cards from everyone you meet (after handing off yours), run home, and mail out those PR packets today!

4. Agents and the Trades

You are ready to get an agent. Are there agents for hosts? Absolutely! There are agencies that specialize in hosts, such as the Paradise Group in Los Angeles, or there are big agencies that have host departments, like ICM or William Morris. As with landing a theatrical agent, it can be difficult to get a host agent. In fact, I am represented by a host manager, not by a host agent. I had a hard time getting one to represent me! I am not using that fact as a way to discourage you, because you may find representation right away. I am actually using it as a tool to encourage you! I currently host two shows: one on ShopNBC and The Vintage Vehicle Show. *For the first job, I was sent out on the audition through my tradeshow agent (see number five, below) and for the second job, I auditioned through* Back Stage West, *believe it or not. There are so many opportunities, and that is why I want you to go out and see the possibilities. Having an agent is a great way to be seen, but it is not the end of the world if you do not find representation right away.*

Here are some agencies to take a look at, if you are seeking host representation. In Los Angeles: ICM, William Morris, Bobby Ball, Paradise Group, Ken Linder & Associates, Abrams Artists, ARL (Abrams, Rubaloff, and Lawrence), and Endeavor. In New York: Don Buchwald and Abrams Artists. This is, of course, a partial list. There may be more agencies on each coast with host departments. I drew from my experience on the audition circuit the names that show up over and over again on the sign-in sheet.

Please do not ignore the power of Back Stage *whether you are in New York or Los Angeles.* Back Stage West *has a comprehensive list of auditions for hosts under the Non-Union TV and Video section. This is a terrific opportunity to add more tape to your reel, gain experience, and network with up-and-coming directors and producers. If you are in the union, get a list of the current cable networks. Read up on who is creating new shows. Did you hear that E! has created a new production company called E! Studios? Did you know that the same conglomerate runs TNN and Nickelodeon? Stay updated on the latest news in the entertainment industry. Read the trades, scan the Internet, and follow up with leads. You never know where that simple little tip will take your career.*

5. Tradeshows

Why am I including this in my host preparation tips? Well, it is how I got my start in this industry, and I believe it is a great stepping-stone to a career as an on-camera host. The tradeshow industry has taken a hit in the past few years due to the economy, but there will always be a need for spokespeople on the tradeshow floor. I began by auditioning for the auto show circuit where I worked as a

Toyota spokesperson for three seasons. It gave me the opportunity to practice my ad-lib and improvisation skills because we were allowed to make up our own scripts. Using bullet points on notecards, I created a different presentation every single time I went up on the stage. I cannot tell you how invaluable the experience was.

The tradeshow industry is a great place to network. It is a wonderful way to get those ear-prompter skills up to par. You will have more distractions and interruptions on the tradeshow floor, so it helps with that "live" element, should you ever do a live show on TV. Often, you have to do a PowerPoint presentation or interact with a video screen using an IFB. These are skills that I honed from within the tradeshow industry that are serving me well today as an on-camera host.

To get involved in this industry, there are tradeshow agents. It is my tradeshow agent that helped me get my job on ShopNBC. Most of the agencies are nationwide to cover both East and West Coast tradeshows. If you want to look into a few, here are some suggestions: Patrick Talent (my agent), Judy Venn & Associates, Alexander & Associates, and Production Plus. Most of these agencies will ease you into tradeshows by having you work as a greeter or host at a booth first, but it is an excellent way to see if you enjoy the work. It is eight hours on your feet and interacting with the public, but know that if you put the time and effort in, this could be a stepping-stone to your on-camera host career.

In closing, remember that hosting is a journey. Results do not happen overnight. So, create three, six, nine, and twelve-month goals to get you that much closer to your dream. Here I am today and I look back on my crazy idea that started in 1998. Who knew I would be a home shopping host? Did I ever think my auto show experience would lead to hosting The Vintage Vehicle Show*? I did not even drive in my nine years living in New York! I am still living by my own five suggestions listed above. I still market myself, I still work the tradeshow circuit, I still update my PR package, and I may even look for agency representation this year. Keep at it... because success happens when preparation meets opportunity!*

—Contributed by Kris Burtt, on-camera host

Stand-up Comedy

Some of the best information I've heard about performance and self-management elements of a comedian's path came from a panel discussion called "Building the Career of the Comedian" sponsored by and for members of the Talent Managers Association. While not everyone who reads this book—or this chapter, for that matter—is pursuing comedy as a career, the advice from these industry experts is relevant to us all, to some degree.

What Are You Looking for in a Comedian?

Bruce Smith, the co-founder of Omnipop Talent Agency and an instructor at UCLA Extension, SAG, and Hollywood Film Festival said simply, "I have no trouble finding talent. Tuning out what everyone else says about the talent is the trick. You have to tune your ear to what is unique, what is specific. A business background would not have helped me at all in this business. It's all about knowing—instinctively—what works."

William Bowley, the former head of the Personal Appearance Department at Don Buchwald and Associates (currently with Power Entertainment) summarized, "When

I'm scouting, I spend five nights a week in comedy clubs. I look for point-of-view, observational humor. The act must have a broad appeal."

Bud Friedman, founder of the legendary Improv Comedy Club, recalled the so-called good ol' days. "In 1963 at the New York Improv, there were hundreds of comedians to look at. Now there are thousands. There's more of everyone now. There's a lot of repeating of the same subject by comedians. It's difficult to find that unique *voice*, but it sparkles when you see it. I look for people speaking in their own voice. It's a rarity, but it's there."

According to Zoe Friedman, Director of Development and Production for Comedy Central's West Coast division (and, yes, Bud Friedman's daughter), her current position introduced a sense of freedom to her scouting. "When I was booking for David Letterman or Craig Kilborn, I was in clubs four or five nights a week, scouting. Now, I go to HBO Workspace or to one-person shows and to clubs. When I'm doing pitches at Comedy Central, I find I have more room to be *blue* than at network, but we don't develop a show around a person's life like networks may do."

Finally, Judy Carter, master teacher, author, and motivational humorist, added her perspective. "I look for people who have a sense of authenticity about themselves. They come from a real place and have passion. All of it must be relatable and strike a chord with everyone. In Los Angeles, we see extreme narcissism. I am horrified by how many people are consumed by their own little world. The 'me, my, I' stuff is so freaking boring!"

Smith added his take on that trend, stating, "The key is creating a world that you can draw the audience into. Your only sin as a comedian is to bore the audience. You cannot screw up by keeping them on the edge of their seats. [Client Christopher] Titus made some club owners nervous when he started out, but he got standing ovations. Our goal—

and Titus has been a client since he was 17 years old—was always going for the long road. That means hooking up with your idols. Who, as comedians, did you love, growing up? Why? Today's comedy is very much about instant gratification. That is limiting."

"I encourage comedians to work on the road," Bowley added. "Live audiences show us what plays well, what's funny region-to-region. You'll only get one or two shots to showcase for the industry, so you need to be ready for that. Road work prepares you for that. You'll have a stigma to overcome, if you're not ready when you showcase. Now, it's hard to promote someone who is on the road, so it's important to be local, especially during pilot season."

"One of the biggest problems," began Zoe Friedman, "is that people are seen too soon out here. You really need to wait until you're ready. I'm a big supporter of the process. You could be ready in a year. Work the craft, cut your teeth in New York. Los Angeles is tough for beginning comics. There's just not a lot of stage time out here."

Bud Friedman concurred. "That's true. In Los Angeles, there's the Improv and two other clubs. In New York, you, as a comic, can go hit eight shows in one night."

"Well, that's the real underbelly of open mics here: the bringer gigs. If you're from a large, Catholic family, you're set! But otherwise, your amount of stage time is based on how many patrons you can bring," Carter explained.

Do Comedians Need Acting Classes?

"Without a doubt," Bowley was quick to insist.

"It depends," Bud Friedman said, though he didn't indicate on what "it" "depends." "I'm a purist, though," he said.

"I still think it would help," Zoe Friedman offered.

Smith explained, "Development people want a story.

Look at *Titus*. Stacy Keach is a great actor. Titus is a good actor for a comic. And he took a lot of acting classes to get good. So many deals get made around a stand-up who had a great seven minutes one night and that's like having had a lucky first date. You don't know what you've signed up for!"

Is a Sketch Comedy Group a Good Way To Showcase Your Skills?

"The drawback to working with four or five other people is: what happens when we just want one? The group dies. It is a wonderful training ground though. I'm in awe of sketch groups," Bud Friedman related.

"Sketch groups are extremely Darwinian," explained Smith. "The Groundlings' program is based on surviving the system. But thinking on your feet is never a bad skill."

Is Writing a Required Skill for Comics?

"In this business, you're thrown against the wall very hard. If you stick, great. If you don't, no one worries about your concussion. It's an ostracizing process," Smith observed. "When you fail, you must retreat, regroup, and come back with a vengeance. One way to do that is by writing. Do what it takes to get writing so that your entire ego isn't wrapped around the performance end of the experience."

"Many of my students go the route of sitcom writing," Carter explained. "Comics are sometimes hired for writing jobs based on their stand-up tapes. There is so much money to make as a comedy writer. I encourage it."

What Should a Comic's Tape Include?

"It doesn't matter," insisted Bowley. "The important

thing is to get the tape made and get it out there."

"Sound quality is more important than video quality. I don't want to hear waitresses over your set. Keep in mind, though, that I won't book you based on a six minute tape. You have to prove you can do 45 minutes to impress me. Headliners bring their openers with them, so I'm not looking to hire someone just for the ten-minute slot up top," shared Bud Friedman.

Zoe Friedman nodded in agreement, adding, "Your tape should have no fast cuts. I want to see the whole set or else I'm wondering what you're cutting out. Of course, there's nothing better than seeing a comic live, but a tape of your work on one of the nightly talk shows will get you in the door with me."

Are Comics Born or Made?

"You can be funny, but it is a craft," Carter began. "We can get any people to be funny for five minutes, but there is a specific structure to the craft. Actors study. Improv performers study. Comics think they don't have to study. You must."

Smith concluded, "If we can't make you funny, you're probably not. I believe that."

Showcases

Let's start by defining the term "showcase," which is often used interchangeably (and incorrectly) with the term "workshop." The casting directors I have interviewed use vocabulary like this: "showcases" are defined as rehearsed, planned, promoted, catered showcases of scenes. Many theatres rent space to performance groups (actors who pool resources to do these things) and others sponsor their own company members' performances. Some acting classes culminate in a showcase performance for agents, managers, and casting directors. No one from the industry is paid to attend these showcases. These folks come for the chance to scout new talent, eat a little food, and take home a press kit filled with headshots and resumés. This is a good use of their time after a busy day at work.

"Workshops" are typically defined as cold reading workshops with casting directors or their associates or even assistants. Actors pay to be in front of these folks, are handed sides, pair up with another actor they may not know, and spend a few minutes rehearsing the scene before presenting it to the casting director. Sometimes the actors receive feedback on their performances, and the casting director leaves with headshots and notes (or provides contact information for follow-up mailings). The casting directors are paid for their time. There is currently a major debate on the legality of these pay-to-play workshops, as many people believe actors should not ever have to pay a person in a position to hire them (that's why you'll see disclaimers in workshop literature stating that the presence of a casting director does not guarantee an opportunity to appear in the casting director's current projects).

My point in clarifying the difference between the two is this: one is much more reputable than the other. When a casting director says in an interview that she attends showcases, she is generally referring to the first definition listed above. Many workshop companies will use the term "showcase" to entice actors into paying to be seen. *Some* acting coaches will provide "incentives" to industry, hoping that such "gifts" will result in high attendance. Generally, these events are held in lower regard, since talent isn't the *only* motivating factor. Just know that casting directors and agents know the difference, and those who say they attend "showcases" do not mean that they do cold reading workshops. Yes, some casting directors do both, but you need to be aware of the difference in these opportunities.

Starting a Group vs. Joining an Existing Group

While many actors see others doing showcases and think, "I could do a better job putting a showcase together," I still recommend that—rather than trying to reinvent the wheel—actors first try to get into an existing showcase group at a reputable space. Certain groups will put up a one-night showcase every few months. Start by asking around (in your classes, at rehearsals, on set, anywhere that you are around other actors who are working) and stay tuned in to what you see and hear. I've heard people talking about being in the diversity showcase over at ABC or being spied at the

HBO Workspace or PS-NBC in New York, for example.

Most major studios have their own performance labs or are in partnership with spaces that do industry showcases. I've seen good self-produced showcases that are quite heavily industry attended at the Stella Adler Theatre, the Elephant Space at the Lillian Theatre, the Egyptian Arena Theatre, and the Luna Café, just to list a few.

Most showcase groups don't advertise because they're not really looking for newbies to join in. So, they rely on word-of-mouth for actors to get involved, or they base selection of new performers on recommendations and referrals from currently-showcasing actors. If you have friends who work at agencies or for casting directors, ask them which showcases receive attention when the flyers and postcards come through.

An existing showcase can be such a closed door that you may have faster results with starting your own showcase, but you must—up front—have the funds to rent space, promote the event, cater it, provide parking, hire a crew to tech the show, and create programs and press kits—without knowing whether you'll have a good turnout. It's hard to say how much industry will turn out for a new showcase event, when it's easier to go with a known commodity. Catch-22, I know.

There is generally a dollar amount attached to an actor's participation in a professional showcase. The exception would be with diversity showcases at the networks or performance spaces that scout and invite talent to participate. But other showcases—even those that have a strong reputation for being a big draw for industry—tend to be (at their origin) actor-produced and that means everyone chips in to make it happen. That cost can vary from about $50 to $200 per participant.

In choosing a group to join, make sure that you've seen a showcase put on by the group before you commit to being a part of the next one. There is no benefit to being part of a sloppy, badly-performed showcase. If industry does turn out, there will be a black mark against all participants if there are too many weak elements to the experience. This also goes for the length of the program. Anything over 75 minutes is going to be too long to keep the interest of most casting directors. They're worn out after a day at the office and don't want to feel punished for having committed to attend a showcase that drags on and on.

Diversity Showcases

If you are a member of a minority group that has been notoriously underrepresented in television and feature films, your time is now! Most studios and networks have regular diversity showcases, and to get involved with those, you simply start by sending your headshot and resumé to the studio or network, attn: Diversity Department.

While most studios and networks hold regular diversity showcases, they aren't very well-publicized to the general population. Most networks have someone who is in charge of *scouting* for diversity showcases. That person (or her team) goes out into clubs to see stand-ups, checks out sketch comedy and improv groups, and takes suggestions from agents who have signed hot new talent. Occasionally, the best and the brightest from certain training programs are invited to participate as well.

Once a group of performers is assembled, the network will invite its producers and writers with development deals in the works to see the talent and—hopefully—make some plans to cast from within that group that was showcased.

NBC has a performance space in New York that is separate from its regular diversity showcases. HBO workspace also is more comprehensive in scope. Most major studios invest in a minimum of twice-yearly showcases, but— as stated above—these are pretty much "invitation only."

When you submit your headshot and resumé to the diversity department, mention in your cover letter that you would like to be considered for the next showcase. Make sure to mention where the scouts can see your work between now and the next showcase (whenever that may be) and then follow up with a flyer for *any* show you're doing, closer to the time you're putting it on.

Should you not fall into a minority group, the network showcases are probably not the right tree up which to bark, so to speak. Instead, you should focus your attention on getting seen in clubs, with performance groups, with improv troupes, and in great plays. Good work will be recognized. Of course, it's important to promote your work (see *Publicity*), so that the network brass will come out to see it. After that, you're more likely to be called in for a preread than invited to participate in a showcase. At least, that's how it's working these days. Next season? Who knows?

Major Success Stories

The show *15 Minutes of FEM* is all women, each is given 15 minutes to do "her thing," and the audience votes for a winner. Everyone in the audience gets to vote, but industry and invited judges get to cast "weighted votes" on the final night. The buzz on these weekly shows is so good that, by the time the judged round comes along, people are wait-listed in hopes of getting in. That becomes an excellent showcase for these women. Was it created as an industry showcase? No. Steve Silverman just wanted a new forum for female performers. Has it become an industry showcase? Definitely. Just this year, the *Best of FEM* (members of four versions of *15 Minutes of FEM*) were asked to showcase for HBO, NBC, and the directors of the Aspen Comedy Festival.

This is in addition to individual invitations the performers have received to casting offices all over town.

Another great example of putting a show on for free (at much cost to yourself, at first) comes from the best one-woman show I have ever seen. Jonna Tamases has been performing *Jonna's Body, Please Hold* for four years throughout Los Angeles. Her willingness to put on this show—about her numerous bouts with cancer and her ability to kick its ass—repeatedly at no charge to attendees is what has led to its recent six-week, fully-produced and completely-funded run (with a plan for national touring to follow). Her free shows during the development process allowed her to invite potential investors—as well as industry—to see the work-in-progress. She believed so strongly in the need for this show that she sunk every penny she had into it, so that she could share it with others. Her personal investment paid off, as members of the industry—and cancer survivors all over the world—have rallied around her and brought this show to its highest production values thus far.

You just never know what the reaction to a mom-and-pop creation will turn out to be! Therefore, you must get involved with something you *really love* and cultivate its reputation!

In Closing

Of course, everyone knows that this business is not about rules or absolutes. There are always magic stories, and that's what keeps the dream alive in so many aspiring performers.

When I first started high school, there was no drama club. So, I helped start one! There are ways to create opportunities to do what we love no matter where we live. Location may be a barrier, but if there is a casting director who really believes in you, you'll be brought in despite the distance. It's not *likely*, but that doesn't mean it's impossible.

If you're not currently living in a major market, look into contests, competitions, scholarships, and everything else that could have high-level scouts open to looking at performers from all areas, but always remember—you should *never* pay to be represented. An agent or manager gets paid only when you do—by commission. Never let your dream get soiled by the greed of others. If you have legitimate talent, there are legitimate representatives eager to sign you.

People who are pegged to one side of their brain tend to have short careers in the industry. They may be very creative, but not have the ability to balance the day-to-day parts of an actor's life and will therefore fizzle out sooner than others may.

Finding Balance

Steve Lockhart, Los Angeles casting director, came up with a delightfully amusing "system" for turning the "I'm an actor" anxiety off.

> *I had a friend who had the problem of reliving auditions over and over after leaving the room, so he went to a hypnotist about it. What a difference! Now he doesn't even know he's an actor unless a key phrase is uttered (which was planted in his mind while he was under hypnosis). Then he stays an actor until a different phrase causes him to forget again.*
> *The phrase that makes him remember he is an actor is: "We'd like to schedule you for an audition." And the phrase that makes him re-forget he's an actor so that he can go about living his life is: "That was nice. Thank you. We'll call you."*

What qualifies as a good year as an actor? Did you do good work? Did you enjoy yourself? Did people ask you to do what you love? Are you gratified by doing what you love? That's a good year. Beyond that, I would say it was a good year if you made enough money to pay for the gas it took to drive to the sets of the films. Or, if you got enough tape to show others your work. What I always used as a benchmark was: "Did I do more work this year than I did last year?" After that answer was always yes, the question became: "Did I earn more money acting this year than I did last year?" Measure your progress, but make sure you always factor in being challenged and enjoying your work!

About the Author

Bonnie Gillespie, originally from Atlanta, Georgia, holds a Master's degree in Journalism from the University of Georgia. Her thesis, *Broadcasting in the Elementary Schools*, is an ethnographic study of live television news broadcasts developed and produced entirely by students.

Bonnie has worked as Instructional Technology Coordinator for Athens Academy and developed extensive staff enrichment courses in the integration of media and technology in education. As Graduate Advisor to WUOG, 90.5fm, Bonnie was named College Radio Advisor of the Year, 1997, by the National Association of College Broadcasters.

Her pursuit of acting brought Bonnie to Los Angeles, where she soon began working as a freelance writer for several publications. Freelance clients have included *Reel Noir*, *Back Stage West*, the Sundance Institute, Roxbury Publishing Company, Hey Anita, and several online publications including ActorsBone.com, ActorPoint.com, WildOgre.com, and EverythingElse.net, the home of her column *It's Like This*, the follow-up to her popular humor column *Don't Get Me Started*.

Bonnie has retired from acting, preferring instead

to write and teach about the craft of casting and the business of acting. Her first book, *Casting Qs: A Collection of Casting Director Interviews* is a top-seller in Los Angeles and has been selected as a textbook for collegiate acting programs nationwide. Bonnie now works as a personal consultant to actors and is a frequent guest speaker at several acting studios and regular free events in Los Angeles. She is also co-founder of the Flickering Image Short Film Festival.

Recently, Bonnie has put her expertise from interviewing over 200 casting directors to the test, having cast the feature *A Dull House* as well as having worked as casting coordinator for the Fox series *Mr. Personality, Paradise Hotel, The Brady Bunch*, and *Project X*. She has provided casting consultant services on several independent projects and is creator and co-host of *Hollywood Happy Hour*; news, schmooze, reviews, and interviews. Bonnie lives in the Hollywood Hills with her fiancé and two cats.

Index

Online Resources

123headshots.com
> Headshot photography by Corey Litwin

123hollywood.com
> Actor websites and hosting

15minutesoffem.com
> One-woman shows, 15 minutes at a time

4entertainmentjobs.com
> Entertainment industry jobs

abcpictures.com
> Lithographic headshot reproductions

acadpd.org
> *Academy Players Directory*

acmecomedy.com
> ACME Improv Comedy Theatre

acop.com
> Online surveys

actingworldbooks.org
> Excellent resource for agency guides

actone.com/janealdermanbio.htm
> Casting director Jane Alderman, CSA

actorpoint.com
> Resources and forums for actors

actors101.com
> Showfax Actors 101 free panels

actorsbone.com
> Free actor discussion forums and actor listings

actorsequity.org
> AEA

actorservices.com
> Services for actors

actorsfund.org
> The Actors' Fund of America

actorsite.com
> ActorSite casting director workshops

actorsnw.com
> Actors Northwest

actorsresource.biz
> Actor's Resource Labels

actors-network.com
> Actors' Network

aftra.org
> AFTRA

agentassociation.com
> Association of Talent Agents

aiastudios.com
> AIA Studios workshops and classes

americantheaterweb.com
> Nationwide theatre locator

artistsalon.com
> Free monthly artist events

askplay.org
> ASK Theatre Projects

auditions.net
> List of auditions

backstage.com
> *Back Stage* and *Back Stage West*

breakdownservices.com/access/awindex.htm
> Actors Access Breakdowns

breakdownservices.com
> Breakdown Services

cafeshops.com
> Put your mug on a mug!

calsnet.net/cricketfeet
> Cricket Feet Calendar

cameronthor.com
> Acting coach Cameron Thor

canadianactor.com
> Canadian Actor Online

castboy.com
> Casting director Billy DaMota, CSA

castingsociety.com
> Casting Society of America

castsag.com
  Resource to find SAG performers
chezjim.com/writing/monologues.html
  Original monologues
cinescape.com
  Film information, news and gossip
clioawards.com
  Award-winning ads
cmeg.com
  Casting director Marki Costello
comedyintensive.com
  Steve Kaplan's stand-up classes
curtainup.com
  Curtain Up features theatre reviews
dailycelebrations.com
  Inspirational quotes
dailynews.com
  Daily News features theatre reviews
dga.org
  Directors Guild of America
donotpay.org
  Do Not Pay (for casting director auditions)
dougwarhit.com
  Acting coach Doug Warhit
dramashop.com
  Hansen Drama Bookstore
eidc.com
  Where things are filming in Los Angeles
entertainmentcareers.net
  Entertainment industry job lists
ent-today.com
  Entertainment Today features theatre reviews
eperformer.com
  Industry news and profiles
erinfiedler.com
  Photographer Erin Fiedler
filmcommissionhq.com
  Links to the world's film commissions
flickeringimage.com
  Film, TV, radio, graphic, web design, and film editing
forums.delphiforums.com/proactors
  Free professional actors resource discussion forum

gobetween.com
> Messenger services

groundlings.com
> Groundlings school and performance group

hahafest.com
> Stand-up resources

hcdonline.com
> *Hollywood Creative Directory*

holdonlog.com
> Excellent organizational system for actors

hollywoodhappyhour.com/hhh
> News, schmooze, reviews, and interviews

hollywoodnetwork.com/callan
> Author K Callan

hollywoodos.com
> HollywoodOS and Extras Casting Guild

hollywoodreporter.com
> *Hollywood Reporter*

hometown.aol.com/castingby
> Casting director Patrick Baca, CSA

hometown.aol.com/lapaladini
> Casting director Mark Paladini, CSA

howardfine.com
> Acting coach Howard Fine

ibdb.com
> Internet Broadway Database

idotvads.com
> Free discussion forum for commercial actors

improv.com
> The Improv Comedy Club

indieclub.com
> Filmmakers networking site

iopinion.com
> Online surveys

jeffreyhornstein.com
> Photographer Jeffrey Hornstein

johnganun.com
> Photographer John Ganun

jonnasbody.com
> *Jonna's Body, Please Hold*

judycarter.com
> Judy Carter's stand-up classes

judykerr.com
>Author Judy Kerr

katselas.com
>Acting coach Milton Katselas

katywallin.com
>Casting director Katy Wallin, CSA

killerreel.com
>Demo reels by Allen Fawcett

krisburtt.com
>On-camera host Kris Burtt

laawc.com
>Los Angeles Actors Workshop Coalition

lacasting.com
>Headshots and resumés online

larryedmunds.com
>Larry Edmunds Bookstore

laweekly.com
>*LA Weekly* includes theatre reviews

learningannex.com
>Offers courses in entertainment studies

lhb-mgt.com
>Talent manager Lola Blank

mapquest.com
>Get directions before you leave for auditions

margiehaber.com
>Acting coach Margie Haber

martincasting.com
>Casting director Melissa Martin, CCDA

members.aol.com/_ht_a/roarkeoo
>Casting director Dino Ladki

members.tripod.com/~chinesecookery
>Los Angeles radio, TV, and newspaper listings

michaeldonovancasting.com
>Casting director Michael Donovan, CSA/CCDA

midwesttalent.com
>Talent manager Betty McCormick Aggas

my8by10.com
>Casting notices and profiles

ncopm.com
>National Conference of Personal Managers

nelsonaspen.com
>Media coach and journalist Nelson Aspen

newscalendar.com/hnc.html
    Hollywood News Calendar
nohola.com
    NoHo>LA features theatre reviews
nycastings.com
    News and resources
omnipop.com
    Bruce Smith's Omnipop Talent Agency
paaw.com
    Performing Arts and Artists Worldwide directory
pfcast.com
    CDs Donald Paul Pemrick, CSA, and Dean Fronk, CSA
photographychick.com
    Photographer Deborah Vancelette
pierodusa.com
    Acting coach Piero Dusa
pioneerdrama.com/stuff/lobby.html
    Catalog of plays
playersdirectory.com
    Academy Players Directory
playersguideny.com
    New York's *Players Directory*
productionweekly.com
    What's in production where
pub130.ezboard.com/bdonedeal
    The Done Deal message boards
quickviewbeseen.com
    See-thru headshot mailers
reproductions.com
    Litho and photo print reproductions
reverseaddress.com
    Look up addresses before doing blind submissions
reviewplays.com
    Theatre reviews
ridinientertainment.com
    Publicist Maryann Ridini
risingashes.com
    Demo reels by Rob Ashe
robmartinphoto.com
    Photographer Rob Martin
sag.org
    SAG

samuelfrench.com
   Samuel French Bookstore
scriptwritersnetwork.com
   Non-profit organization for screenwriters
seatfiller.com
   Work as a seat-filler at award shows
secondcity.com
   Second City companies and classes
showbizmonster.com
   Labels, resource guides, forums
showfax.com
   Source for audition sides
skirball.org
   Skirball Cultural Center
soapcity.com
   Soap opera news, fansites, and discussion forums
stageagent.com
   Nationwide audition information
stand-upcomedy.com
   Greg Dean's stand-up classes
stephonfuller.actorsite.com
   Actor Stephon Fuller
stuart411.com
   Casting director Stuart Stone, CCDA
studiotalentgroup.com
   Talent managers Phil Brock and Kathy Boole
take1filmbooks.com
   Take One! Bookstore
talentmanagers.org
   Talent Managers Association
terryberlandcasting.com
   Casting director Terry Berland
theactorsoffice.com
   Organizational software for actors
theatrela.org
   Theatre League Alliance
theatresports.com
   Improv and TheatreSports
thebuzznyc.com
   Members-only casting listings
thecastlist.com
   Fee-based database of actors

thedailycall.com
> Wireless entertainment job alerts

thejobfactory.com
> The Job Factory

thomas.com
> *Thomas Bros. Guide*

tolucantimes.com
> *The Tolucan Times* feature theatre reviews

tvtattle.com
> Weblog of TV news and criticism

tvtix.com
> Studio audience tickets

ubcptalentonline.com
> British Canadian branch of ACTRA

uclaextension.org
> Department of Entertainment Studies

us.imdb.com
> Internet Movie Database

variety.com
> *Daily Variety*

watchreels.com
> Library of demo reels

wga.org
> Writers Guild of America

whorepresents.net
> Find out who represents whom

wif.org
> Women in Film

wildogre.com
> Canadian actors discussion forum and resources

wolfesden.net
> Free actor discussion board courtesy of Sterling Wolfe

writersblocpresents.com
> Events for writers

youngplaywrights.com
> Workshop performances by young playwrights

Recommended Reading

Before even heading to Los Angeles to give acting a go, aspiring actors should skim, if not memorize, the chapters of the following essential books and guides.

Acting in Commercials: A Guide to Auditioning and Performing on Camera by Joan See. If you're planning on doing any commercial acting, and you're coming to Los Angeles from a market where commercials aren't where you're getting work already, you'll need to check this book out for its tips including on-camera acting techniques, the difference between commercial and theatrical auditions and bookings, and ad copy as scene work.

Acting Is Everything: An Actor's Guidebook for a Successful Career in Los Angeles by Judy Kerr. Judy's book is a major must-have. I am very excited that she asked me to contribute to its tenth edition. This has long been considered the leading book on the business of acting in Los Angeles.

Acting Out: Your Personal Coach to a Money-Making Career in Television Commercials by Stuart Stone, CCDA and Dennis Bailey. Start with the basics and zoom through to pro-level commercial work with this handy guidebook.

An Actor Succeeds: Career Management for the Actor by Terrance Hines and Suzanne Vaughan. I like this book, even though it's a bit out of date, because it is the first of its kind, featuring Q&A formatted interviews with casting directors, agents, managers, a writer-producer, an attorney, an accountant, and a publicist. When I first read this book, I was amazed that there was no "industry standard" when it comes to sending unsolicited headshots, demo reel formatting, or audition etiquette. It's nice to know that every casting director is different, when it comes to likes and dislikes. That way, as a self-marketing actor, you can do what makes you comfortable and know that there will be casting directors with whom your methods click. Much of the work I did in *Casting Qs* came from the early influence of this book.

The Actor's Encyclopedia of Casting Directors: Conversations with Over 100 Casting Directors on How to Get the Job by Karen Kondazian. Another book of Q&A formatted interviews with casting directors in Los Angeles, but this one includes photographs. I'm a big fan of knowing what casting directors look like, as I think we often place too much value on schmoozing the "stars" at parties, when we should be chatting up the casting directors, perhaps.

The Agencies: What the Actor Needs to Know by Lawrence Parke is regularly updated with the most current contact information for agencies, their union affiliation status, and a list of what "types" are currently targeted by each agency. This book is a must-have for the actor looking to change or acquire representation.

The Artist's Way: A Spiritual Path to Higher Creativity by Julia Cameron is a book that includes daily and weekly exercises to nurture your inner artist. If you have any creative blocks whatsoever, this book has practical—although touchy-feely—advice on putting healing in motion, so that you can be free to create with passion.

Audition: Everything an Actor Needs To Know To Get the Part by Michael Shurtleff. Craft is key. Get your audition skills up to snuff with the granddaddy of all audition technique books.

Be a TV Game Show Winner! by Marla Schram Schwartz. An often-overlooked way to get TV exposure, and make some good money while you're at it, the game show has long been a popular outlet for aspiring actors. There's more to booking a game show than just sending in a headshot and resumé. While game shows encourage actors to apply (union status doesn't matter), the producers will want you to not "technically" be an actor. This book includes information on how to be chosen, how to win, how to handle the IRS, and how to be chosen again and again to appear on game shows and win fabulous prizes!

Book the Job: 143 Things Actors Need To Know To Make It Happen by acting coach Doug Warhit includes information on how to cry on cue, work your close-up, and be funny (even if you're not) by focusing on the immediate task, rather than the big picture.

Breakdown Services' CD Directory is a quarterly-updated guide to CSA, CCDA, and independent casting directors. The neighborhood breakdown of casting director locations is especially useful for the actor who chooses to drop off headshots without zigzagging across town. While the directory is published quarterly, there is an update generated every week. Because many casting directors work out of production offices and do not keep regular, permanent office space, this feature is especially important for the actor who needs to keep tabs on those casting directors. Subscribers receive those updates by mail or by email, for the duration of the subscription term.

Breaking into Commercials: The Complete Guide to Marketing Yourself, Auditioning to Win, and Getting the Job by Terry Berland and Deborah Ouellette. A comprehensive guide to working in commercials, including information on the headshots and resumés best suited for commercial actors, audition protocol, and details of the commercial shoot, plus specific information on voiceovers and crossing over from modeling to acting using commercials as the path.

Casting Qs: A Collection of Casting Director Interviews by... yours truly. I'm biased, of course, but this is currently the most up-to-date, comprehensive casting director interview book out there.

CSA's Casting By.... This is like the IMDB.com of casting directors in book form: a list of which CSA members cast what projects and who produced those projects as well.

Extra Work for Brain Surgeons by Hollywood OS is still one of my favorite guides for actors of all aspirations (not just those specializing in extra work). It's hip, useful, entertaining, and informative in its presentation of extras casting services, pay rates, union details, and on-set vocabulary.

The Film Actor's Complete Career Guide: A Complete, Step-by-Step Checklist of all the Things Actors Seeking Professional Film and Television Careers Can and Should Do, When and How To Do Them, from the Very First Steps to Top Starring Careers by Lawrence Parke. This book includes essential information on where to live, traps to avoid, where to study acting, resources, interacting with those who've seen and heard it all by the time you've just learned the vocabulary, unions, promotion, resumé formatting, and blank forms for your own record-keeping. This is another must-have, for sure.

Getting the Part: 33 Professional Casting Directors Tell You How To Get Work in Theatre, Films, Commercials, and TV by Judith Searle. Another collection of those great Q&A formatted interviews with casting directors in Los Angeles and New York. Anyone who plans to get in front of casting directors regularly needs to do as much homework as possible to learn who these people are.

Holdon Log, the Only All-in-One Audition Organizer, is something every actor needs, in order to set up an organizational system for cataloging auditions. Many actors gloss over the importance of record-keeping, but this log will assist even the most right-brained actor with keeping track of mileage, sides, wardrobe, and post-audition follow-up.

How To Be a Working Actor: The Insider's Guide To Finding Jobs in Theatre, Film, and Television by Mari Lyn Henry and Lynne Rogers. You'll learn there's a big difference between the actor and the *working* actor.

How To Get the Part Without Falling Apart by Margie Haber. One of the most respected acting coaches in the business lays down the how-*not*-to-screw-up info in a fun-to-read guide.

How To Make It in Hollywood: Everything You Need to Know About Agents, Managers, Lawyers, Chutzpah, Schmoozing, the Casting Couch, Godfather Calls, Rhino Skin, Handling Rejection, How To Be Lucky, and All the Steps You Need To Take To Achieve the Success You Deserve by Linda Buzzell. This book includes, well, everything. The author is both a psychotherapist and career counselor who focuses on "all the steps you need to take to achieve the success you deserve" in this easy-to-read guide to the industry. For out-of-towners headed to Los Angeles, this book is a must-have for orientation.

How To Make Yourself (or Anyone Else) Famous: The Secrets of a Professional Publicist by Gloria Michels. This book may be out-of-date, but I like it because it includes checklists for fame-making formulas, ten commandments for dealing with the media, and extensive recommended reading on the subject. Any book along these lines would be a nice addition to an actor's bookcase.

How To Work a Room: Learn the Strategies of Savvy Socializing for Business and Personal Success by Susan RoAne is a very useful book for those actors who may struggle with the schmoozing part of the job. This book includes practical information on how to overcome roadblocks to an essential element of being a professional actor in Los Angeles: networking. I couldn't remember names when I started reading this book. Now, I never forget anyone or anything that was said in an exchange with anyone. Working a room is a skill you can develop and one that you will enjoy having, once you've overcome the aversion to schmoozing. You're going to have to do it, so get prepared.

I Could Do Anything If I Only Knew What It Was: How To Discover What you Really Want and How To Get It by Barbara Sher and Barbara Smith. If you're struggling with exactly what your dream life looks like, start by taking a step back and analyzing it with this book.

Impro: Improvisation and the Theatre by Keith Johnstone is a guide to improvisational storytelling, an important, but often-overlooked tool to enhance traditional acting techniques. Craft-specific information, exercises, and techniques add to core acting curriculum and audition confidence.

L.A. from A to Z: The Actor's Guide To Surviving and Succeeding in Los Angeles by Thomas Mills. Tom is the former guru to thousands of readers of *Back Stage West.* In his popular "Tombudsman" column, he answered reader mail about all things acting every week for nearly ten years.

The Los Angeles Agent Book: Get the Agent You Need for the Career You Want by K Callan. The eighth edition, published in 2003, is the most up-to-date incarnation of this book. I like it most for its interviews with many, many agents, which give a glimpse into the personality and business ethics of these usually inaccessible folks.

Next! An Actor's Guide To Auditioning by Ellie Kanner, CSA, and Paul Benz, CSA. This is a how-to-audition guide written by working casting directors.

So You Want To Be an Actor... Act Like One by Jerold Franks is about to hit bookstores in an updated printing. The former CSA president covers topics from marketing tools to dealing with rejection, and has added a section on the debate over paid casting director workshops and the licensing of teachers.

Survival Jobs: 154 Ways To Make Money While Pursuing Your Dreams by Deborah Jacobson is a book I have recommended to everyone I know. It details amazingly innovative ideas for ways to make money without having to take a nine-to-five job in Los Angeles. If you're tired of the "golden handcuffs" of a fulltime job, this book will open doors for you, big time!

The Tightwad Gazette: Promoting Thrift as a Viable Alternative Lifestyle by Amy Dacyczyn. A great guide (in fact, a series of books) to practical, easily-integrated lifestyle tips for saving money at every turn.

Wishcraft: How To Get What You Really Want by Barbara Sher. Another in the line of *The Artist's Way* style books, this one includes strategies to overcoming fear, goal setting, progress checklists, and exercises to improve the speed of your manifestation. If you lack focus and are good with journal-based activities, this is a great tool.

Your Film Acting Career: How To Break Into the Movies & TV and Survive in Hollywood by M.K. Lewis and Rosemary R. Lewis. The book that many people in the industry have called "the actor's bible," this one includes nuts and bolts information on living in Los Angeles and taking care of the business of acting (and being a working actor).

Other Titles from Cricket Feet Publishing

Casting Qs
A Collection of Casting Director Interviews
© 2003 $21.95 ISBN 0-9723019-3-3
by Bonnie Gillespie

Acting Out
Your Personal Coach to a Money-Making
Career in Television Commercials
© 2003 $16.95 ISBN 0-9723019-5-X
by Stuart Stone, CCDA and Dennis Bailey

Casting Calendar
An Actor's Datebook and Action Log
by Bonnie Gillespie
Spring 2004

Cricket Feet Publishing Title Order Form

Online and Credit Card Orders: visit any major online bookseller or CricketFeet.com.

Postal Orders: send this form with check or money order to
Cricket Feet Publishing
P.O. Box 1417
Hollywood, CA 90028
Please do not send cash.

Check all books you are ordering at this time:
- ❑ *Casting Qs: A Collection of Casting Director Interviews*
$21.95
- ❑ *Acting Out: Your Personal Coach to a Money-Making Career in Television Commercials* $16.95
- ❑ *Self-Management for Actors: Getting Down to (Show) Business* $18.95

Name: _____
Address: _____
City: _____ State: _____ Zip: _____
Telephone: _____
Email Address: _____

Please call 323.871.1331 to arrange for bulk discounts to bookstores and educational facilities.

Sales tax: please add 8.25% tax for products shipped to California addresses.

Shipping: United States: $3 for first book, $2 for each additional book; International: $10 for first book, $4 for each additional book.

Payment (in U.S. dollars):
Check or Money Order Total Enclosed: _____

❑

Check here if you would like to be added to our mailing list for notification of future publications, speaking engagements, and other promotional activities.